What people are saying about

Resetting Our Future
SMART Futures for a Flourishing World

This intriguing title for a book is based on a tantalizing concept and the vision through the lenses of a futurist. Claire Nelson establishes a Smart Futures Framework that projects how we will live, work and play in a new hypervigilant world. It takes us through the niches of a world of planetary species, a result of race-based legal systems. It vividly illustrates how a proxy of global consciousness has evolved in "tribes" and "meshworks" of relationships. Its narrative is about th~ ~ny of a world whereby billions are being spent on ~ ~te a new home on other planets having faile~ ~~equity gaps on earth. The ultimate ~ ~k is that it provides bridges of ~ ~
Ambassador Eddie ~ ~or, University of Guyana

This visionary synthesis of our current global situation uses the tools of science fiction, prophecy, and policy analysis in combination to make a compelling description of where we are, where we could get to in terms of making a good future for humanity, and also, crucially, how to get there. It's a wonderfully entertaining and informative book — a call to action!
Kim Stanley Robinson, Science Fiction Author

For years, the Americano-Caribbean "White House Champion of Change," Claire Nelson, has advocated for a more sustainable, inclusive way of development. Her new book is another brilliant, inspiring Call for Action, that stands out from the mass of post-COVID anticipatory works: a "must read" for all decision makers for its clear, well-grounded and documented (the metrics of the engineer!) description of where we are right now and where we are heading in the next years. More broadly, I recommend it to everyone wishing to lucidly face the very challenges every human being on Earth ought to address if we are to survive as a species: overcome our toxic tendency to endlessly fight our fellow man; move to and master the *glocal* level, combining instead of opposing our global and local identities; and transform yourself, whoever you are, into a SMART agent of change.

Fabienne GOUX-BAUDIMENT, Ph.D., CEO, proGective, Foresight Consulting Company, Paris

A view of humanity from the future, and an engaging and thought-provoking discourse, Dr. Claire takes us into numerous scenarios in making our future SMART, while keeping the discussion threads grounded to the current challenges faced by the human race. An invigorating read that pushes the mind to think about better lives and opportunities for humanity and our future. A must read for anyone who cares about our human condition and believes in our capacity for change and is looking for guidance to direct the path.

Deepa Naik, Cofounder Cogitari, Co-CEO Humans for AI, India

Now, just when we need it, Claire A. Nelson offers us a "magical mystery tour" that opens up new horizons, evokes both the sources of hope and despair, and finally, master story-teller that she is, inspires us to seek beyond the confines of yesterday's imagination. I recommend this book to everyone, from the aficionado of wild fiction to the ardent scenario planner. Enjoy, explore, learn, encounter the provocations needed at a time of fluidity in order to recognize the anticipatory assumptions that lock us in place and those that do not. Thank you, Claire, for this gift.

Riel Miller, Ph.D., Head of Futures Literacy, UNESCO, Paris

In this fictionalized account of past, present, and future, what emerges from Dr. Nelson is a set of design truths that should capture our attention and activate us to mobilize. She weaves a compelling perspective on our collective future as a single human race and establishes a visionary and principled foundation of sustainability, morality, agency, resilience, and technology. The resulting framework is both intellectually enlightening and inspirationally moving.

Kemper Lewis, Ph.D., Dean, School of Engineering, University of Buffalo, New York

This book is a unique seed of hope accompanied by exclusive nourishment of Dr. Claire A. Nelson's matchless vision, and scintillating imagination. She boldly forecasts a future out to Y3K. She then works the projection back to today with witty, creative fiction on one hand; on the other, crisp, data-based, harshly realistic presentation of the current state and projections onto coming decades. The result is this audacious volume that bonds us all at the primal level of chills that accurate prophesies send down our spine. Yet it maintains a gentle sense of humor poking fun at, while warning in no uncertain terms against, our short sighted, misguided priorities.

Sirin Tekinay, Ph.D., Chair, Global Engineering Deans Council

"Tribes of the World, coordinate!" is my five-word summary of Claire Nelson's enthusiastic book *Smart Futures for a Flourishing World*. She combines passion, insight and knowledge into a powerful narrative of a way forward, out of the social and environmental mess we, as hegemonic species and global market capitalist society, have created the past half-millennium.

Martin Bohle, Sc.D., affiliate of the Ronin Institute for Independent Scholarship (Montclair, NJ, USA) and Edgeryders (Brussels, Belgium)

Claire Nelson has a knack for thinking differently than I do, and that makes reading her work incredibly valuable for helping to solve problems. In *Smart Futures for a Flourishing World*, she takes us to the future and back with stories that illustrate the storms of the present and illuminate paths of hope for the future. She brings her Caribbean lilt to the stories, making the stories at once magical and thought-provoking. Whether you are thinking about what you can do about climate change or poverty, or you are considering how we can colonize space without making more of a mess this book will be an inspiration.
Lise Laurin, CEO, EarthShift Global

If you fancy Science Fiction, if you are interested in long term futures, if you think that conventional futures reasoning lacks fantasy, this is a book for you. In *Smart Futures for a Flourishing World,* you meet an imaginative power that goes beyond the most of expected horizons. In this fairy tale from the long and not so long distant future, Claire Nelson, not only forces us to think through some basic social political perspectives, she also bring in surprising socio-technological ideas in a way that both stimulate you to further reading, and makes you both comfortable and uncomfortable with our current society.
Erik F. Øverland, Ph.D., President, World Futures Studies Federation

There is no doubt that the ongoing COVID-19 pandemic marks a momentous occasion in the twenty-first century and indeed, in global history. The pandemic has transformed our lives in myriad ways and on multiple levels resulting, according to Dr. Nelson, in a "pregnant pause." Millions of persons have been infected by the coronavirus, many of which have been fatal; masked faces; social distancing; constant sanitization, remote work and learning became norm. The pandemic has not only re-shaped life as we once knew it, but more importantly, it has re-defined our future, forcing us to "cross the chasm from the future we wanted to the future we now have."

I commend Dr. Claire Nelson, an outstanding member of the Jamaican Diaspora in the United States, for writing this book, *Smart Futures for a Flourishing World*, which walks us through this evolving shift in global consciousness. She cleverly combines humor and satire in order to convey a message to her readers that a flourishing future is not only desirable, but entirely possible. For Dr. Nelson, a futurist, sustainability engineer, social entrepreneur, storyteller and recipient of multiple awards, the publication of the book, *Smart Futures for a Flourishing World*, is one in a series of her many accomplishments. As Ambassador of Jamaica to the United States, I am truly proud of the remarkable contribution that Dr. Nelson has made over the years to the Jamaican community in the DMV and indeed the wider United States. I congratulate her on this important feat.

H.E. Audrey Marks, Ambassador of Jamaica to the USA

Dr. Nelson asks us to re-imagine and write the future we want. Can we save ourselves from ourselves? Dr. Nelson warns, we must devise or recognize the paradigm shift or the future we find ourselves in will be dictated by the gods. I was pleasantly surprised by this book which feels like three books and easily transports the reader back and forth in time. I highly recommend it as a great addition to our tool box for decolonizing our thinking, and making the much-needed paradigm shift.

Yul Anderson, Founder, African American Futures Society

My main concern about the future is linked to the changes that I have seen just in my lifetime. When I taught Environmental Science, the Green Revolution of 1945–50 was touted in our Miller textbook as the turning point in agriculture during the twentieth century. However, since 1950, the world's population has tripled. Perhaps the SMART Futures framework could help paint a clearer picture, of how our future society will be more integrated, color-blind and diversified.

Tom Valone, Ph.D., President, Integrity Research Institute, USA.

Resetting Our Future

SMART Futures for a Flourishing World

A Paradigm Shift for Achieving Global Sustainability

RESETTING OUR FUTURE

SMART Futures for a Flourishing World

A Paradigm Shift for Achieving Global Sustainability

Claire A. Nelson

CHANGEMAKERS
BOOKS

Winchester, UK
Washington, USA

JOHN HUNT PUBLISHING

First published by Changemakers Books, 2021
Changemakers Books is an imprint of John Hunt Publishing Ltd., No. 3 East Street,
Alresford, Hampshire SO24 9EE, UK
office@jhpbooks.com
www.johnhuntpublishing.com
www.changemakers-books.com

For distributor details and how to order please visit the 'Ordering' section on our website.

Text copyright: Claire A. Nelson 2021
Cover Art by Bal Anthony De Jorge

ISBN: 978 1 78904 775 2
978 1 78904 776 9 (ebook)
Library of Congress Control Number: 2020945769

A CIP catalogue record for this book is available from the British Library.

Design: Stuart Davies

UK: Printed and bound by CPI Group (UK) Ltd, Croydon, CR0 4YY
Printed in North America by CPI GPS partners

We operate a distinctive and ethical publishing philosophy in
all areas of our business, from our global network of authors to
production and worldwide distribution.

Contents

The *Resetting Our Future* Series

At this critical moment of history, with a pandemic raging, we have the rare opportunity for a Great Reset – to choose a different future. This series provides a platform for pragmatic thought leaders to share their vision for change based on their deep expertise. For communities and nations struggling to cope with the crisis, these books will provide a burst of hope and energy to help us take the first difficult steps towards a better future.

– Tim Ward, publisher, Changemakers Books

What if Solving the Climate Crisis Is Simple?
Tom Bowman, President of Bowman Change, Inc., and writing-team lead for the U.S. ACE National Strategic Planning Framework

Zero Waste Living, the 80/20 Way
The Busy Person's Guide to a Lighter Footprint
Stephanie Miller, Founder of Zero Waste in DC, and former Director, IFC Climate Business Department

A Chicken Can't Lay a Duck Egg
How COVID-19 Can Solve the Climate Crisis
Graeme Maxton, (former Secretary-General of the Club of Rome), and Bernice Maxton-Lee (former Director, Jane Goodall Institute)

A Global Playbook for the Next Pandemic
Anne Kabagambe, former World Bank Executive Director

Power Switch
How We Can Reverse Extreme Inequality
Paul O'Brien, Executive Director, Amnesty International USA

Impact ED
How Community College Entrepreneurship Creates Equity and Prosperity
Rebecca Corbin (President & CEO, National Association of Community College Entrepreneurship), Andrew Gold and Mary Beth Kerly (both business faculty, Hillsborough Community College)

Empowering Climate Action in the United States
Tom Bowman (President of Bowman Change, Inc.) and Deb Morrison (Learning Scientist, University of Washington)

Learning from Tomorrow
Using Strategic Foresight to Prepare for the Next Big Disruption
Bart Édes, former North American Representative, Asian Development Bank

Cut Super Climate Pollutants, Now!
The Ozone Treaty's Urgent Lessons for Speeding Up Climate Action
Alan Miller (former World Bank representative for global climate negotiations), Durwood Zaelke (President and founder, the Institute for Governance & Sustainable Development) and Stephen O. Andersen (former Director of Strategic Climate Projects at the Environmental Protection Agency)

Resetting Our Future: Long Haul COVID: A Survivor's Guide
Transform Your Pain & Find Your Way Forward
Dr. Joseph J. Trunzo (Professor of Psychology and Department Chair at Bryant University), and Julie Luongo (author of *The Hard Way*).

SMART Futures for a Flourishing World
A Paradigm Shift for Achieving Global Sustainability
Dr. Claire Nelson, Chief Visionary Officer and Lead Futurist,
The Futures Forum

The Rebalancing Act
Charting a New Path to Lead, Parent, Partner, and Thrive
Monica Brand, Lisa Neuberger & Wendy Teleki

Resetting the Table
Nicole Civita (Vice President of Strategic Initiatives at Sterling
College, Ethics Transformation in Food Systems) and Michelle
Auerbach

www.ResettingOurFuture.com

Today we are faced with a challenge that calls for a shift in our thinking, so that humanity stops threatening its life-support system. We are called to assist the Earth to heal her wounds and, in the process, heal our own – indeed to embrace the whole of creation in all its diversity, beauty and wonder. Recognizing that sustainable development, democracy and peace are indivisible is an idea whose time has come.
Wangari Maathi, Nobel Peace Prize Winner

There seem to be solid biological reasons why we are the way we are. If there weren't, the cycles wouldn't keep replaying. The human species is a kind of animal, of course. But we can do something no other animal species has ever had the option to do. We can choose: We can go on building and destroying until we either destroy ourselves or destroy the ability of our world to sustain us. Or we can make something more of ourselves.
Octavia Butler, Science Fiction Hall of Fame

No matter who we are or what we look like or what we may believe, it is both possible and, more importantly, it becomes powerful to come together in common purpose and common effort.
Oprah Winfrey

Preface

Like Octavia Butler said, "I have a huge and savage conscience that won't let me get away with things" and "why can't I do what others have done – ignore the obvious. Live a normal life. It's hard enough just to do that in this world." But I believe in our power to choose to become the change we want to see. And that belief initiates and guides my actions. I had to conquer my fear and answer the call to write the SMART Futures book when it came. I see it as my offering on the altar of our need to change our course as a species. As my dish in the banquet of life that is ever unfolding. The book was supposed to be a short, quick guide to the SMART Futures Framework as I explain it. But, the storyteller-shero in me got ahold of the plot, and refused to let my engineer-self go forward without her prognostications on what might be said by our future descendants if we were able to get the story right now. I must admit that the idea of journeying as far afield as to the year 3000 CE was nerve-wracking. Time travel to 2050 was the furthest I had ever been. Who would go with me? And would we arrive alive? But then I remembered that long ago, more than 3,000 years ago, there was Namaah. Namaah – Noah's wife who helped provision the ark for the journey through the existential flood of that era. And I thought surely if she was able to believe in and pack for the unseen future, then so could I. Moreover, I knew I could always call on Anansi for help. Some of you might ask. Anansi? Who? Why? Anansi, is the Trickster God of the Ashanti peoples. Anansi often takes the shape of a spider and is considered to be the god of all knowledge of stories. One of the most important characters of West African mythology, Anansi traveled through time and space to the Caribbean with the enslaved Africans to ensure they maintained their connection to their Godself. Anansi is well known for how he brought wisdom to the world, even if it was only by accident. Anansi has been my faithful companion on the road to conjuring change, and I was sure that Anansi could help to make the future clearer to me. It is a truism that every shero worth her weight, needs to pack properly for the journey. Thankfully, I unearthed some musical gems that served to feed my soul along the way. From Bob Marley to Jimmy Cliff, to Steel Pulse and Chronixx, the rhythms kept my blood singing through the slog of night and weary days. You can check out the playlist in the notes. These could well be called the anthems for the future we want. The future is embedded in the landscape around us and, all of us who see that there is work to be done must do our part. This call to make a shift is my doing what I can right now. And, if and when I can do more, I will. I hope you will join me.

Foreword

by Thomas Lovejoy

The pandemic has changed our world. Lives have been lost. Livelihoods as well. Far too many face urgent problems of health and economic security, but almost all of us are reinventing our lives in one way or another. Meeting the immediate needs of the less fortunate is obviously a priority, and a big one. But beyond those compassionate imperatives, there is also tremendous opportunity for what some people are calling a "Great Reset." This series of books, Resetting Our Future, is designed to provide pragmatic visionary ideas and stimulate a fundamental rethink of the future of humanity, nature and the economy.

I find myself thinking about my parents, who had lived through the Second World War and the Great Depression and am still impressed by the sense of frugality they had attained. When packages arrived in the mail, my father would save the paper and string; he did it so systematically I don't recall our ever having to buy string. Our diets were more careful: whether it could be afforded or not, beef was restricted to once a week. When aluminum foil — the great boon to the kitchen — appeared, we used and washed it repeatedly until it fell apart. Bottles, whether Coca-Cola or milk, were recycled.

Waste was consciously avoided. My childhood task was to put out the trash; what goes out of my backdoor today is an unnecessary multiple of that. At least some of it now goes to recycling but a lot more should surely be possible.

There was also a widespread sense of service to a larger community. Military service was required of all. But there was also the Civilian Conservation Corps, which had provided jobs and repaired the ecological destruction that had generated the Dust Bowl. The Kennedy administration introduced the Peace

Corps and the President's phrase "Ask not what your country can do for you but what you can do for your country" still resonates in our minds.

There had been antecedents, but in the 1970s there was a global awakening about a growing environmental crisis. In 1972, The United Nations held its first conference on the environment at Stockholm. Most of the modern US institutions and laws about environment were established under moderate Republican administrations (Nixon and Ford). Environment was seen not just as appealing to "greenies" but also as a thoughtful conservative's issue. The largest meeting of Heads of State in history, the Earth Summit, took place in Rio de Janeiro in 1992 and three international conventions—climate change, biodiversity (on which I was consulted) and desertification—came into existence.

But three things changed. First, there now are three times as many people alive today as when I was born and each new person deserves a minimum quality of life. Second, the sense of frugality was succeeded by a growing appetite for affluence and an overall attitude of entitlement. And third, conservative political advisors found advantage in demonizing the environment as comity vanished from the political dialogue.

Insufficient progress has brought humanity and the environment to a crisis state. The CO_2 level in the atmosphere at 415 ppm (parts per million) is way beyond a non-disruptive level around 350 ppm. (The pre-industrial level was 280 ppm.)

Human impacts on nature and biodiversity are not just confined to climate change. Those impacts will not produce just a long slide of continuous degradation. The pandemic is a direct result of intrusion upon, and destruction of, nature as well as wild-animal trade and markets. The scientific body of the UN Convention on Biological Diversity warned in 2020 that we could lose a million species unless there are major changes in human interactions with nature.

We still can turn those situations around. Ecosystem restoration at scale could pull carbon back out of the atmosphere for a soft landing at 1.5 degrees of warming (at 350 ppm), hand in hand with a rapid halt in production and use of fossil fuels. The Amazon tipping point where its hydrological cycle would fail to provide enough rain to maintain the forest in southern and eastern Amazonia can be solved with major reforestation. The oceans' biology is struggling with increasing acidity, warming and ubiquitous pollution with plastics: addressing climate change can lower the first two and efforts to remove plastics from our waste stream can improve the latter.

Indisputably, we need a major reset in our economies, what we produce, and what we consume. We exist on an amazing living planet, with a biological profusion that can provide humanity a cornucopia of benefits—and more that science has yet to reveal—and all of it is automatically recyclable because nature is very good at that. Scientists have determined that we can, in fact, feed all the people on the planet, and the couple billion more who may come, by a combination of selective improvements of productivity, eliminating food waste and altering our diets (which our doctors have been advising us to do anyway).

The Resetting Our Future series is intended to help people think about various ways of economic and social rebuilding that will support humanity for the long term. There is no single way to do this and there is plenty of room for creativity in the process, but nature with its capacity for recovery and for recycling can provide us with much inspiration, including ways beyond our current ability to imagine.

Ecosystems do recover from shocks, but the bigger the shock, the more complicated recovery can be. At the end of the Cretaceous period (66 million years ago) a gigantic meteor slammed into the Caribbean near the Yucatan and threw up so much dust and debris into the atmosphere that much of biodiversity perished. It was *sayonara* for the dinosaurs; their only surviving close relatives were precursors to modern day birds. It certainly was not a good time for life on Earth.

The clear lesson of the pandemic is that it makes no sense to generate a global crisis and then hope for a miracle. We are lucky to have the pandemic help us reset our relation to the Living Planet as a whole. We already have building blocks like the United Nations Sustainable Development Goals and various environmental conventions to help us think through more effective goals and targets. The imperative is to rebuild with humility and imagination, while always conscious of the health of the living planet on which we have the joy and privilege to exist.

Dr. Thomas E. Lovejoy is Professor of Environmental Science and Policy at George Mason University and a Senior Fellow at the United Nations Foundation. A world-renowned conservation biologist, Dr. Lovejoy introduced the term "biological diversity" to the scientific community.

Acknowledgements

Give Thanks! This book would not have been possible without the vision of Changemakers Books and John Hunt Publishing that decided that the world needed to have diverse voices joining in the collective search for a better future for all humanity. For sure, there are many who contributed to the execution and existence of this book. I must begin with Rick Smyre, from Communities of the Future, who placed my name on the table and brought me into the circle. I also owe an enormous debt of gratitude to my three muses — Chris Daley, Ian Edwards, and Kim John Williams — who allowed me to borrow their ears in order to help me to find my voice. They spent many hours and late nights listening to me speak the vision that is the Smart Futures Framework into being and gave freely of their own talent to explore the nuances of my ideas and push me to clarify concepts and to calibrate ideas more precisely. Without them, this process would have been more painful.

It has been a joy to practice my passion for global evolutionary change through dialogue with others who are genuinely interested in making change happen. I am indeed grateful to the many friends and colleagues in the Institute of Caribbean Studies and The Futures Forum who have allowed me the privilege of a practice, that has served as my personal learning laboratory. Through these spaces, I have been able to seed and birth the construct of the SMART Futures Framework, beginning with my first foray into the world of futures back in 1999 during my sojourn at the Inter-American Development Bank, where I labored to breathe futures thinking to the development finance community. Thus, to my booster team, Carlos M. Jarque Uribe, Mark Wenner, and Jerry Butler, I am much obliged for serving as godfathers.

To my personal chorus — Karema Daley, Deneise Francis

and Dr. Shelly Cameron thank you for encouraging me to come out of hiding and write a book (instead of running for political office). I must make special mention of Choirmaster and Yoke Fellow, Dr. Nsombi Jaja, whose unwavering faith in my abilities has been the wind beneath my wings. I can't thank her enough for staking her reputation in serving as midwife to so many of my dreams and my personal development over some forty-plus years. She has been an untiring torchbearer for my walk in the world.

I want to acknowledge my debt to my editor Michelle Auerbach, for her support and guidance, and especially for finding a way to allow the characters who came to life in the writing of this non-fiction book to find safe harbor. Indeed, she helped make the tedium of the edit, and the re-edit a pleasure. I must also thank Bal Anthony De Jorge for his artistry in bringing my concept of the cover art to life. Likewise, my thanks to all the unseen hands that help make this book a reality — Tom Bowman and Nick Welsh for cover design, Krystina Kellingley (copyedit and proofreading), Stuart Davis (book design), and Andrew Wells (production manager).

To Tim Ward, publisher of Changemakers Books, who was inspired to invite me to be part of the crew in the Resetting our Future Series, I offer heartfelt thanks. I have been benefitted by his counsel during the process of writing the book, and his patience through the final stages of completing this project, given the many departures I took from his prescribed route. His vision of creating this author cohort is refreshing for writing is largely a solitary sport. Indeed, I am grateful to all the other authors in the Resetting Our Future Series, for agreeing to walk together in constructing alternate paths to the future.

Finally, I want to thank my life partner, Dwight Beckford, for being the spiritual ballast that I need to carry out the everyday business of living while trying to answer the call to ministry as an activist in this world. Indeed, he is to be commended for tolerating my absences from the dining table and for putting up with my various time travel escapades when I did surface to join him in the discourse of polite dining. This book is for my mother who taught me to believe in myself, and in the power of God to use even those who others may see as less than. I am as God made me – a conjurer of change. "Hineni." Here I am. Give Thanks.

Introduction

I am a futurist and sustainability engineer with over 30 years of experience doing international development work. I've always brought to the table, my sensibilities as a woman who grew up in 1960s Jamaican elementary school reciting a national pledge that states: "Before God and All mankind / I pledge the love and loyalty of my heart / The wisdom and courage of my mind / The strength and vigor of my body/ in the service of my fellow citizens / I promise to stand up for Justice Brotherhood and Peace / to work diligently and creatively / To think generously and honestly, so that / Jamaica may, under God, increase in beauty, fellowship and prosperity / and play her part in advancing the welfare of the whole human race."

I admit that these days I replace the word brotherhood with the more politically correct and inclusive word "humanitism" but that pledge made me the little girl who, despite a terrible stutter, was recognized as the champion of the underdog and official crier against status quo adult oppression. It set me on the path to becoming a global citizen.

Twice in my life I have been a movement starter and from that experience I have learned the questions we need to ask ourselves and those became the SMART Futures Framework about which you will learn in this book. And, both times it has required that I consciously let go the notion of control to give the movement the opportunities to live freely and grow in the visions of those who see themselves in it. When I began the development with equity movement to champion the cause of blacks in Latin America, all I had was a vision. My contributions to crafting policy for the international financial institutions and UN World Conference Against Racism have led to results I could only dream of. I had to learn to live with the idea that power had to be shared for it to be sustained beyond my immediate sphere of influence.

Likewise, in midwifing the National Caribbean American Heritage Month movement, again I had to learn that the vision of creating a place for Caribbean immigrants' contributions to America to be recognized nationally demanded that I let go of the impetus to control the process and the flow. Big visions and ideas demand a meshwork of leaders and followers picking up a thread and weaving their own vision of the design into the tapestry.

I have had the experience of being a minority voice – the only Black woman in the room for much of my adult life whether it be my engineering classes, or in the hallways of the Washington establishments that prognosticate the future for the world. Indeed, it is a fact that much of what we experience in the world today has been and is being prescribed by the leadership elite across the western educated industrialized rich developed countries. We all know, absenting the Queen and a sprinkling of political unicorns, usually the leaders in that space are male and pale. Since there seems to be no seat for me at the table, I've taken a leaf from the book of my shero the late great Shirley Chisholm – a daughter of Caribbean immigrants to America who decided so many years ago to run for the President of the USA on the democratic party ticket – and I've decided to bring my folding chair. We are at a crossroads where humanity has serious choices to make and even the masters in the echo chambers of the global leadership estates such as the World Economic Forum now admit they don't really know the answers either. Part of the reason they don't know is that they are not asking the right questions, the SMART Futures questions.

The future is shared space. And I think it's time that we all get the opportunity to throw down at the feast of ideas that will constitute the life of the party or rather this party called life. As a futurist, sustainability engineer and development with equity advocate, as a social entrepreneur, as a storyteller, I do believe that this book is my story to tell.

"How might we make a paradigm shift to create a flourishing world that fosters inclusive prosperity?" is the question this book strives to answer and I feel fit for the purpose.

I am at heart, a storyteller. It used to be that I separated my engineering self from storytelling self. However, once I experienced success in using storytelling as a tool for workshop report on "How Peace Came to the World" at a 1997 Salzburg Seminar on Race and Ethnicity, I did research on storytelling. I have come to discover that stories are how we experience reality, and that storytelling is a recognized as a means for changing minds and hearts. I think by changing the stories we are telling about the future, we can change our ideas about who we are and how we function and so make a paradigm shift possible.

To support the SMART Futures framework, I've chosen to weave stories that borrow from the notion that as humans we are embedded in myths of our creation that inform our worldview and thus our systems of governments and laws and regulations. I have crafted stories from the aspirational future, which paint positivist pictures of the future. I do not believe in Utopia, but I am chagrined by the numerous dystopian tales of who we will become out there littering our thought waves. I have chosen to begin in the year 3000, which is outside of our time, because I want to make sure that we understand that life will go on way beyond our ability to conceptualize what that might look like with any accuracy. I use 2100 as another point of departure because the children who were born in the year 2020 – the year of the COVIDemic will only be 80 in that year. Just imagine what they will be speaking about on December 31, 2099. A look back at the last century – which is to say the first century of this third millennium. If this COVID-19 Pandemic is to become the gestation center of the birth of a new idea of who we might become as humans, then we must begin to impregnate the possibilities with our visions of the futures we want. My last story is set in 2030 because that is the time and place that is closest to us and because there is the beginning of a shared global vision of the future we would want to have achieved in the 17 United Nations global Sustainable Development Goals.

I would like the reader to leave this book, knowing that change is possible. With the SMART Futures Framework, change is imminent. I'd like you to become futures literate and to use that literacy about the futures we share to inform their practice of life and thus help to improve how we operate Spaceship Earth. I want you to see beyond the veil of what is and understand more about how we come to this pass – this crossroads of crises – so that you can think the SMART Futures way and do the SMART thing. I would like you to leave this book, feeling optimistic about our capacity to be the change we want to see. There are many of us dreamers, marching for and protesting against, and generally working our fingers to the bone to do what we can to save the thing in the world we are called to save. I'm hoping that these stories I tell leave you feeling curious and open, if not exhilarated, and certainly less anxious about what lies ahead. Our words become our stories and our stories matter. I say this with conviction based on my own personal story, as somebody who was destined by authorities to be a mouse to be ignored or stepped on, but who saw myself as a lion and who thus became the mouse that roared and crafted a story that made me a conjurer of change.

Prologue

A View of Humanity from the Dreaming

How Humans Were Saved from Extinction: Is Anansi "Mek" It

"KRIK!" (And you say "KRAK!")

The story is told that back in the day, long before humans spread across the Milky Way and began traveling to other galaxies, back in the primitive days when they were only on Earth and were called Homo sapiens sapiens, which stood for doubly wise humans, even as their primitive brains were not yet fully able to understand the true nature of time, humans lived in fear of each other. Imagine... in those days, humans fought incessantly. As much as sixty million people killed because of one war. Even after they discovered how to split the atom, dropped two nuclear bombs and finally formed the global organization called the United Nations to prevent mutually assured self-destruction, humans kept on fighting. Humans always seemed to find something to fight about.

"KRIK!" (And you say "KRAK!")

Even after they had learned how to decode the genome and had invented technologies that could take them to explore the Earth's Moon and settle on other planets in their solar system. Even after they invented probes that could travel to their Sun and powerful telescopes that showed them the billions of stars in their Galaxy the Milky Way, and that there were billions of Galaxies, and that the Universe of Galaxies was still expanding, they were still starting fights over small-small insults because of over-large egos. They fought over which God was more powerful. They tried to kill off the Goddesses. They fought because in some Tribes they wanted women to be equal, while some Tribes did not value women. They fought because of perceived differences in access to the Gods, because of skin color, and eye shape and hair texture. Even after they discovered over 4,000 exoplanets beyond the Earth's Solar System and had begun the hunt for Earth 2.0, they were still fighting.

"KRIK!" (And you say "KRAK!")

Humans! Instead of working together to help solve the problems they faced like figuring out how to slow down the warming of the planet and stop the wasting of resources and cut the greed that was causing them to use up the resources of the Earth at a faster rate than which Pacha Mama could replenish it – they were fighting as if the Earth and the heavens belonged to them. They had not yet learned that humans belong to the Earth, that humans belong to the Cosmos. Not the other way around. They were on a collision course with the will of the Gods. So, Chaos (the God of the Void before Creation) decided to call a Summit of the Pantheon of the Gods.

"KRIK!" (And you say "KRAK!")

From all corners of the Universe the Gods and Goddesses came, riding on beams of light, to attend to the Universal Conclave on Earth Affairs. From those who took care of the Americas, the representatives included: Nanabozho of the Ojibwe, Hopi Grandmother Gogyeng Sowuhti, Cōātlīcue of the Aztec and Viracocha of the Inca. From the Gods of the Near East came Atum in Ennead, whose semen becomes the primal component of the universe, Ptah who created the universe by the Word, and Neith, who wove the universe and existence into being on her loom. From Asia came Esege Malan from Mongolia, Kamuy from the Ainu, who built the world on the back of a trout and Izanagi and Izanami-no-Mikoto who churned the ocean with a spear, creating the islands of Japan. We had Brahma and Shiva from the Hindus. From Europe, representatives to the Great Conclave included Odin of the Norse, Zeus of the Greeks, and the goddess Arianrhod of the Celts. From the Oceania sector, came Anjea of the Murri peoples, Makemake of Rapa Nui mythology, Ranginui – the Sky Father, and Papatūānuku, the Earth Mother of the Māori. From Africa came Mbombo of the Bakuba, Oludumare of the Yoruba, Unkulunkulu of the Zulu, and Nyame of the Akan. All of them came from far and wide in the twinkling of time for when Chaos called, no one played deaf.

"KRIK!" *(And you say "KRAK!")*

When Anansi, *chief interlocutor of human affairs, heard about the Universal Conclave of the Pantheon of the Gods on Earth Affairs to address the Homo Deus Conundrum, he decided that he had to be there. But how? The Conclave was for the Gods, and he was really just a demi-semi-right-hand-assistant to Nyame, so, Anansi worked hard to convince Nyame that it was best for him Nyame to take Anansi along so that he Nyame would not have to deal with the pesky details of ensuring follow up after the Conclave, should any action have to be taken. After all, he Nyame, had so much to do, that he should not have to take his precious time dealing with details best left to lesser beings such as himself Anansi. And that is how Anansi came to be there.*

" KRIK!" *(And you say "KRAK!")*

Well, *the gathering began with the usual greetings and salutations with news from across the multiverse of time and Space until the Conclave was called to order. Cronus entered the time on the Scroll of Life and the Norns, all three sisters – Urðr who saw fate, Verðandi who watched the present and Skuld who scanned the future – there at the Well of Urd that holds our destiny beneath Yggdrasil, the great tree that stands at the center of the universe, started weaving a new pattern on the tapestry of life.*

Chaos *hailed, "Kindred! I have gathered you together to discuss what to do with the problems the humans are causing on Earth. Pacha Mama has cried out to us for help. Despite the many warnings she has sent – flood, hurricanes, wildfires, hailstorms, earthquakes, typhoons all in one solar year – humans don't seem to be taking heed. She needs our help. Frankly, I am of the mind to do them in and start over." There was an eruption of responses. "Do them in?" asked Makemake "Do Them In!" declared Shiva. "Do Them Over?" Ranginui was exasperated. Viracocha intoned with disgust, "I can't believe we are here again. I had to do them over before. I sent a flood to destroy the first set. I made some new ones and placed them all around and gave them everything they needed. But still, they continued with the*

14

*fighting, and I was going to do them in again and start over once
more, when some of them sent a delegation to plead their case and
they pleaded so prettily that I felt that I had to give them a pass for
effort." The opinions on the pronouncement were loud and varied.
"Start Again?" "Do Over." "Do Them In." "Another Flood." "Not
a Flood… A Fire!" "An Asteroid!" "A Pandemic!" "A Solar Storm."
"Maybe we should wait." "Do Them In."*

"ORDER!" thundered Chaos. He loved the word "order."

*In the silence that followed, Anansi frantically interjected. For he,
Anansi, had been listening with increasing horror to the conversation.
He was indeed fond of the creatures that kept him entertained. But in
truth, he was more concerned about his own future. With no humans,
he could no longer be the Chief Interlocutor of the Department of
Human Affairs. He would no longer hold sway to instigate, castigate
and promulgate in the matters of Earth. In the silence, he whispered
in his most ingratiatingly humble voice, "Excuse me Great Ones." It
was the voice he used when we wanted to get something for nothing.
"Who whimpers? That is not the voice of a God." Chaos snarled.
Nyame responded, "It's my Court Jester, Anansi. Let him speak."
Anansi was a bit chuffed to hear Nyame refer to him as a Court Jester
but he knew enough to not let anything but a smile lie on his face.
"Great Ones," Anansi began, "I am well aware that the human race
can be trying. For I spend much time with them daily and I know what
havoc they have been wreaking on your wondrous creations. However,
Great Ones, Wise Ones, do they not deserve justice? I beg permission
to speak in their defense." A chorus of voices rose from the assembly.
"Justice." "Maat." "Kaulike." "Whakawa." "Order," growled Chaos.*

*"Great Ones," Anansi began again. "I have three questions. How
is it you expect to make them in your likeness and then not expect
them to try to make great things like you? Why did you not give them
eyes like the dragonfly, the memory of an elephant, or the lifeline of the
great bowhead whales? What if I could prove that the human race will
save the Earth if only so they can save themselves?"*

A murmur of indrawn breaths arose.

"Hmm. And how would you prove that?" asked Chaos.

"Well, I would travel through 'Everywhen' – where past, present and future exist – and bring you artifacts that prove that the human race will find its way forward," said Anansi. Chaos replied, "Hmm. Alright You have three cycles of the Earth on its axis." Three days? Anansi maintained a cool front but inside his heart was beating like the sound of the storm rain on dry earth. He may need three days just to figure out a plan.

"Great Ones," he said, "Given that you the Gods created the Earth in seven days, surely you can give me, a mere Court Jester seven days to find and bring back proof that the human race will spare the Earth and save themselves. I ask this in the name of Shamash."

"Justice." "Maat." "Kaulike." "Whakawa." "Themis."

"Omoikane." The chorus of voices thundered across the stars and asteroids tumbled in the wake of the sound. Chaos held up his hand and decreed, "It is decided. The Conclave has spoken. Anansi, we give you seven days to go into the Everywhen and bring us back evidence as to how your human friends spare the Earth and so save themselves from extinction. If you fail, Pacha Mama will have her wish. For she is a jewel in the crown of creation, and she must live." And so, Anansi set off on a journey to the Everywhen – where past, present and future exist – to search Everywhere for evidence that could save Everyone.

"KRIK!" (And You Say "KRAK!")

Day One
The Year 3000
Anansi Scopes Out Artifacts from the Year 3000

We stand for a single Exoteranet where all humanity across the galaxy has equal access to knowledge and ideas. We stand for the principle for interdependence knowing that we exist as interbeings. We are StarSeed.

The Manifesto for The Third Millennium

A Voicenote

January 1, 3000
Ambassador Dr. Araminta Agyeman, Commissioner for Interplanetary Peace for the United Peoples Interplanetary Federation
Diplomatic Dispatch UTC 00:01 01.01.3000

Tonight, I begin the next leg of my trek. This is not my first time traveling the circuit across all of our settlements to Alpha Centauri, but it will likely be the last time and the best time, since my mission is to finalize arrangements for the 100ᵗʰ Anniversary of the Space Goodwill Games scheduled for 3035 CE. The implants that allow my brain to take in information at the speed of light and my body to withstand the forces of Space travel are wearing down, and at 120 Earth years, I have decided not to take the upgrades needed to remain on the mission field.

But first, tonight, I will enjoy the festivities planned with my clan here in LunarVille. I will spend some time with the youth interested in joining the United Peoples Inter-Planetary Federation as Ambassadors on the History Holodeck visiting the years 1000 and 2000. That is always fun, to look back and see how far we have come technologically. It will nourish me for my journey.

It is a privilege to be one of the one hundred and fifty ambassadors for the Inter-Planetary Federation. When I leave LunarVille tonight, I am headed to the interstellar research outpost on Phobos, Mars' Moon. The gravity chamber there gives us trans-humans the week we need to adjust to extremely low gravity. My Aide-de-Camp, Serena, who is a Theta-Class Android, will do much of the prep work while the three of us trans-humans on the mission decompress. I am traveling with the Vice Chair of the Space Olympics Board and one of foremost Terraforming Experts. Phobos wants to show that they could host one of the games here. It's been five years since I was there last. At the time they were in the process of building low gravity terrariums and if I recall, trying to grow genetically modified ginkgo and turmeric to supplement their diets. The reports uploaded to the Exoteranet have shown minimal progress but with the interplanetary network of scientists they have access to, it is only a matter of time. To think, we went from hoping *to land on the moon in 1969 to* living *there in just 100 years and now we are all over. I seem to have gotten side-tracked on this entry. I'm meant to keep them short and pointed, but I am still mostly human. I get caught up in the story.*

Just imagine. Almost one thousand years ago, when the Breakthrough Starshot project was announced (specifically in the year 2016 of the Gregorian Calendar) to launch a mission to Alpha Centauri, Earth's nearest star system, in the year 2069 in honor of the 100th year anniversary of the Apollo 11 moon landing, it was considered just another Space fanatic's dream fueled by childhood dreams of a television show called Star Trek. *This was way before the International Space Solidarity Agency was formed following the passage of the Charter on Space in 2059, which gave all objects in Space corporate personhood and gave the Just Futures Alliance the right to police and manage utilization of Space by all. Back then in the twentieth century, every country on Earth had its own Agency. There was some collaboration, but the mindset was still one of individualism. Perhaps the dream may have died a natural death had it not been for the fact that there was a billionaire who wanted to be in the Space race* and the fact that the year 2020 changed everything.

It was the year of the Great Transition as the history books call it. There was a global pandemic which led to the birth of the Ubuntu Alliance. At that time, using the fastest spacecraft technologies at hand, the NASA-Germany Helios probes, traveling at 250,000 kilometers per hour, the 4.4 light years distance between Earth and Alpha Centauri (which is nearly 40 trillion kilometers) would have taken 18,000 years. That did not stop the dream, for humans in pursuit of a powerful dream are unstoppable. They needed an energy breakthrough. Something that could cut the travel time to decades. Now, at the same time there was a group of fringe scientists who were passionate about alternate energy and who were almost fanatic on the search for research funding for Zero Point Energy (ZPE) and the development of the Casimir Engine. Their interests were to converge.

The goal of the first mission was to make a fly-by of and possibly photograph any planets that might exist in the system such as the Proxima Centauri b, that had already been identified by the European Southern Observatory. The design proposed was a spacecraft-on-a-chip weighing less than 1 gram with large, featherweight light-sails, that would be boosted to more than 20% of light-speed by an enormous array of high-powered lasers on Earth. They had ruled out chemical, solar-electric, and nuclear-thermal technologies the race also proposed to explore nuclear fusion and the electromagnetic ramjet.

Meanwhile, around that time the seeds of a growing grassroots movement to promote the sustainability of Space and the just use of Space was coalescing. By the year 2030, the UPSTARTS, which was short for the United Planetary Society to Assure the Rights to Space had emerged solidly against nuclear anything in Space was born. Once word got out, they began campaigning against the construction of high-powered lasers from Earth into Space, using the SMART Futures doctrine which was the Magna Carta of the day for sustainable and regenerative design and as proponents of the wildly popular Space Goodwill Games, which had been launched in 2035, their opinions held sway globally.

So that when the solar storm of 2039 hit, which was more powerful than the one that caused the 1989 Québec and US northeast blackout, and as presaged by scientists, caused massive problems as satellites and power systems were damaged and much of the world was shut down for weeks. This propelled to the forefront the need for a distributive energy system that could be used both on Earth and in Space. Enter the ZPE and the Casimir Engine into popular consciousness. And the rest is history.

And today on Earth, the headquarters of the Interplanetary Space Weather Prediction Center continually monitors the sun from both Space and the Earth. Now when a big coronal mass ejection (CME) is on its way, it is possible for satellites to shut their systems off briefly and Earth-based power grids can be reconfigured to provide extra grounding. This is why in 2359 — five hundred years after the Carrington Event in 1859, the first solar storm observed and recorded which had a coronal mass ejection (CME) that traveled to Earth in only 17 hours, rather than the usual three or four days – we were more prepared. The paradigm shift to SMART design in the twenty-first century had laid the foundations for a new way of thinking that led to the adoption of distributed energy systems that allowed us to repair tears in the fabric of the Exoteranet.

I never cease to wonder about the genius of those early pioneers who did this without the benefit of AI and the Exoteranet that we have instant access to. And we are finding so many known unknowns and noting that there are most likely many unknown unknowns. As we travel the Milky Way, we are doing our best not to make the same mistakes we made on Earth. Though we managed to heal some of the wounds we made in the last millennium, we are mindful that the quest for thrival, amidst the challenges we face as a species and our insatiable dreams have kept us venturing forth in deep humility. For now, we understand the galaxy does not belong to us, we belong to the galaxy.

Chapter 1

What Is the Challenge We Face?

In Ghana, fantasy coffin design is high art. For families who believe that life transcends death and that the deceased will continue with their afterlife profession, their dead have to be buried in something that represents their life. These caskets which have been carved in the form of cars, shoes, lions, airplanes and the like have been the subject of many feature stories and documentaries. Given the need to bury the images and hopes that we might have had of the future in our pre-COVID world, I have been wondering how we might borrow from this tradition to help us commemorate this transition with utmost pomp and circumstance. What ritual and design would symbolize the death of the old order of our oil-frenzied lopsided world and put to rest in peace the hallowed econo-gospel of the gross domestic product (GDP) and all other symbols of a worldview that no longer serve us? How can we best signal our knowing that a new world is waiting to be birthed?

Where Are We Now?

It is 2021 CE in the Gregorian Calendar. It is the Year of The Ox or 4719 in the Chinese Calendar, 1442 AH in the Islamic year. Before the global lockdown, 2020 was being touted as the year of plenty-plenty. We had grand plans for our various endeavors and a heady vision of what successful outputs and outcomes would look like in our lives. Some of us had five-year dreams, and some of us – the globalists – had etched in our psyche our dreams for the year 2030. Now here we are – at a very pregnant pause. We seem to be all asking the question "what's next?" What will be the shape of the new normal in our shared futures? How will we share our planet, our humanity, our rulebooks, and our decision-making architecture?

One thing is certain, all 7.8 billion of us in the human family are living in a volatile, uncertain, complex, and ambiguous – or as we say in short, a VUCA world. Exponential change is taking place across all systems – economic, environmental, political, social, and technological. And, it is said that humanity has ushered the Age of the Anthropocene.

The current epoch is called the Holocene, which began 11,700 years ago after the last major Ice Age. But more recently, we have transitioned to what is being called the Anthropocene Age (derived from the Greek words *anthropo* for "man," and *cene* for "new") because it was noted that human activity has started to have a significant impact on the planet's climate and ecosystems. Now, back to the main story.

Some theorize that the Age of the Anthropocene began at the start of the Industrial Revolution of the eighteenth century when human activity began to significantly impact carbon and methane in the Earth's atmosphere. Others believe that the Age began in 1945, when humans tested the first atomic bomb, then bombed Hiroshima and Nagasaki, Japan, because resulting radioactive particles were detected in soil samples globally. What is not debated is that the events on Bikini Atoll marked a turning point in our evolution as the only species capable of self-annihilation. And so, we have continued.

According to the World Economic Forum, we now live in an Industry 4.0 world. We've come a long way from the first Industrial Revolution of the eighteenth century which used steam power and mechanical systems to adopt manufacturing processes that enabled the railways, mass transportation and created the deplorable working conditions that led to the formation of labor unions. The second Industrial Revolution, in the nineteenth century, saw advancements in the iron, steel, coal industries, telecommunications and transportation sectors, electrical-powered assembly lines and the birth of mass production which, among other things, helped make the automobile more affordable for the average family. The third Industrial Revolution in the 1960s, often called the digital revolution, brought the introduction of computer-controlled systems and devices, simple automation, increased mass production and the birth of ARPANET (used by the military), the forerunner of the internet, which saw the light in the early 1990s. The Fourth Industrial Revolution is characterized by a fusion of technologies that blur the lines between the physical, digital, and biological spheres. It amplifies the internet with its possibilities of billions of people connected by mobile devices holding unprecedented processing power and storage capacity and multiplies emerging technology breakthroughs in fields such as artificial intelligence, robotics, the Internet of Things, autonomous vehicles, 3-D printing, nanotechnology, biotechnology, materials science, energy storage, and quantum computing. We are experiencing exponential transformation of production systems, management, governance, services, work, and customer experience in every industry in every country.

What's Driving This Change?

Three of the global megatrends driving the need for exponential change are population, accelerating technology/connectedness, and climate change/natural resources stress. With the advancements we saw in our four Industrial Revolutions we should be able to meet the challenge, and yet we are not.

Population

The 2020 world population is 7.8 billion up from 6.1 billion in 2000. For the first time, the majority of people in the world live in cities. As of 2018, 55% of the world's population lives in urban areas, and that proportion is expected to increase to 68%. That is another 2.5 billion people by 2050. Close to 90% of this increase will take place in Asia and Africa. Africa and Asia are home to nearly 90% of the global rural population estimated at 3.4 billion. Tokyo is the world's largest city with 37 million inhabitants, followed by New Delhi with 29 million, Shanghai with 26 million, and Mexico City and São Paulo, each with around 22 million inhabitants. By 2030, the world will have 43 megacities with more than 10 million inhabitants, most of them in developing regions. According to 2019 UN estimates, there are 1.2 billion persons between ages 15 and 24 years, or around one in every six persons worldwide, and this is projected to grow to 1.3 billion by 2030. Where are these youths? Mostly in Central and Southern Asia (361 million), followed by Eastern and South-Eastern Asia (307 million) and sub-Saharan Africa (211 million). This is in contrast to the Western educated independent rich developed (WEIRD) countries which are aging, and in the low-fertility countries of Asia and Europe, overall population sizes are stagnant or declining. A global aspiration for a WEIRD "middleclass" standard lifestyle is cause for concern. According to the Global Footprint Network, we are using more natural resources (Ecological Footprint) than our ecosystems can regenerate (biocapacity). We are running an "ecological deficit" which as of 2019, was 1.6 Earths in a given year. Pacha Mama is not amused. How will we change our economic activities and aspirations so as to avoid a self-inflicted population disaster is the question?

Technology

There are some 4.6 billion internet users in the world today, on an average day, over 185 billion emails are sent, close to 5 million blog posts are written, over 555 million tweets are sent, and we have "googled" over 5 billion searches. In 2020, there are 4.8 billion mobile phone users of which 3.5 billion are smartphones. That is 44.8 percent of the world, or in other words, more than four out of every ten people in the world are currently equipped with a smartphone that has more computing power than the original IBM mainframe computers, which were the size of a car, costing $3.5 million each, that were used to make independent computations and maintain communication between Earth and lunar landers back in the days of the Apollo missions. As expected, smartphone ownership is significantly higher across advanced economies. An average of 76 percent of adults in these countries report owning a smartphone, with the highest usage coming from South Korea, where nearly every adult (95 percent) is a smartphone user.

Whereas, in emerging economies, due to the high rates of poverty, smartphones are unaffordable and beyond the reach of many. In Latin America and Africa, just around 45 percent of adults own a smartphone, and many rural areas are yet to be connected. Yet, mobile money solutions such as MPESA and Money on Mobile has already transformed the lives of millions of unbanked in Kenya and India respectively. And, in spite of internet access gaps, social media has turned Gen Z digital natives which make up 30 percent of the global population into a new globally connected generation despite the uneven distribution of technology.

Climate Change and Natural Resource Stress

The Greenland ice sheet and Arctic Sea ice are melting. Permafrost (that layer of frozen soil that covers 25 percent of the northern hemisphere and acts like a freezer) is shrinking. This is possibly releasing long dormant microbes, ancient carbon, poisonous mercury, and soil that has been locked in place, and exposing frozen plants that have not seen the sun in 45,000 years, as radiocarbon dating research indicates.

Melting ice caps on Mount Everest, Mount Kilimanjaro, the Alps, and the Quelccaya in the Peruvian Andes, give rise to fears of floods and lack of water at the same time. Meanwhile, islands are disappearing. Like Isle de Jean Charles in Louisiana which has lost 98% of its land and most of its population to rising sea levels. This is just one of the many islands being washed away from the Chesapeake Bay to the Pacific Sea, where Kiribati, a country made up of 32 atolls, has seen soil eroded, damaged food crops, seawater flooded freshwater ponds and residents forced to retreat. We have watched a town called Paradise burn in California and millions of square miles of land in Australia and Brazil go up in flames. Hurricanes have destroyed the economies of the Bahamas and the US Virgin Islands; floods have laid waste to Benin and Bangladesh. In climate circles, the projection is that at the current rate, the fuse on the climate bomb will explode around the year 2050, if nothing is done to slow the warming of our carbon heavy lifestyle.

In 2019, there were a total of 409 natural disaster events (weather and earthquakes) around the world. The combined economic losses (insured and uninsured) cataloged by insurance broker Aon was valued at $232 billion (2019 USD) of which $229 billion came from weather-related disasters. The last decade 2010–2019 was the costliest among the last three decades – typhoons, flooding, hurricanes, cyclones, drought, heatwaves, wildfires, windstorms from Australia through Central and Western Europe, China, India, Japan, Malawi, Spain, the USA to Zimbabwe. We cannot escape the weather or weather disasters linked to the exponential increase in population and economic activities that have stressed the natural ecosystem beyond its ability to self-regulate.

There are nine planetary boundaries that scientists have defined as a safe operating space wherein humanity can continue to thrive. The boundaries set the limits for: climate change, ocean acidification, stratospheric ozone depletion, disruption of the nitrogen and phosphorus cycles, global freshwater use, land use changes, biodiversity loss, aerosol loading in the atmosphere, and chemical pollution.

We are fast approaching the boundaries for freshwater use, land use changes, ocean acidification, and the phosphorus cycle.

We have already crossed the boundaries for climate change, interference with the nitrogen cycle, biodiversity loss. The last two do not make headline news but in terms of biodiversity loss over the last four hundred years, we have driven at least 680 vertebrate species to extinction. Today we have some 8 million number of animal and plant species on Earth (including 5.5 million insect species) of which up to 1 million are threatened with extinction in coming decades with more than 40% of amphibian species and a guestimate of around 10% of insects threatened with extinction. And while we all have our quarrels with "creepy-crawly" insects, let us be clear that we cannot live without them. Bees and other pollinators such as butterflies, birds and bats affect 35% of the world's crop production, increasing outputs of 87% of the leading food crops worldwide, plus many plant-derived medicines.

No wonder the children are marching for justice. Up until the twentieth century, most existential or global catastrophic risks were natural, such as the super-volcanoes or asteroid impacts that led to mass extinctions millions of years ago. Our recent technological advances have brought with us unforeseen "gifts" to fear such as nuclear energy accident or war leading to nuclear winter; biotechnology accident arising from cloning, gene splicing and a host of other genetic science advancements which could lead to genetic diversity loss or manufactured pandemics; and runaway artificial intelligence (AI). Toxic chemicals are leaching into our ground waters and micro-plastic is to be found not only in the infamous plastic ocean patch but also in the flesh of the fish we consume alongside mercury. To add insult to injury, even our green visions have a brown underbelly. As it turns out solar panels often contain lead, cadmium, antimony, and other toxic chemicals that cannot be removed without breaking apart the entire panel. The glass often cannot be recycled as float glass due to impurities. The International Renewable Energy Agency (IRENA) estimated there was about 250,000 metric tonnes of toxic solar panel waste in the world at the 2016 and that this amount could reach 78 million metric tonnes by 2050. Where is it going to go? We still view natural resources as abundant and cheap in large part because we do not count the true lifecycle costs from cradle to grave. And worse, given that much of the mining and resources industry is taking place in the backwoods of developing countries, we don't pay much attention to the fact that the hunt for the resources that feed our comfortable lifestyles, often lie at the heart of wars and civil strife.

What Is Driving Conflict and Its Comrades?

Mineral Greed

The minerals of our everyday life such as cobalt, coltan, copper, uranium and gold have fueled many civil and interstate wars in Africa. Sometimes these minerals provide rebel groups with cash to purchase arms, and sometimes they provide governments with the resources to repress their people. Not to call names – mining and resource companies, traders, smugglers, corrupt local officials, arms dealers, transport operators and mercenaries are part of the "cheap oil and minerals" value chain. There have been countless UN reports and resolutions as well as NGO studies that have helped raise public awareness and catalyzed global advocacy movements in defense of the communities or the Earth itself.

That smartphone you use every day works because of coltan. That's coltan – not Coltrane – a dull black metallic ore consisting of two minerals, columbite and tantalite, which refines to a heat-resistant powder (tantalum) that holds a high electrical charge. Tantalum capacitors are a vital part of mobile phones, laptops, pagers, electric cars, optical equipment, smart bomb guidance systems, medical equipment, and surgical appliances such as bone replacements, binding agents for muscles and connectors for damaged nerves, since it does not cause an immune response in people. Coltan is the new oil. It is a conflict mineral. Value-chain of illicit coltan is relabeled and sent to legitimate smelters, processed, made into capacitors, and sold to electronics companies – whose names we know. In Africa, foreign corporations exploit countries for minerals without paying billions of dollars in taxes contributing to their underdevelopment. Men, women and children as young as seven, are forced at gunpoint, and beaten by security guards, to mine the coltan using picks and shovels. They toil for 12 hours a day, in intense heat, carrying back-breaking loads, without protective gear for a dollar or two a day to provide the key components for $600 smartphones. Coltan, unlike conflict diamonds, has no "geo-fingerprints" so it is difficult to control its flow and keep conflict minerals out of the legitimate stream. Efforts by American and European companies to secure certification of the substance, has proven difficult, since China and India, the world's largest coltan users, fail to participate in the process and in America, the "corporate" lobby has been chipping away at Dodd-Frank Act passed by Congress and signed by President Obama in 2010 which requires manufacturers to know the source of materials in their supply chain. Our hands are not clean. Resource wars fuel some of the military expenditure of states in Africa which grew by 1.5 percent to an estimated $41.2 billion in 2019 owing to several ongoing conflicts – Burkina Faso to Cameroon, Central African Republic, Chad, DRC, Mali, Niger, Nigeria, Somalia, South Sudan and Uganda.

Military Proliferation

Total global military expenditure rose to $1917 billion (that is almost $2 trillion) in 2019, according to new data from the Stockholm International Peace Research Institute (SIPRI). What if this money were used instead to pay for education? Consider that $1 trillion could pay for 8.3 million students to attend a four-year college course costing $30K a year instead of financing multiple conflicts and wars arising from ethnic tensions, increased nationalism from global powers, transnational terror organizations and other non-state violent agents.

Ethnic Conflict

In Europe and Eurasia, we find ongoing conflict in Ukraine, as well as between Turkey and Armed Kurdish Groups, and the Nagorno-Karabakh Conflict. In Asia, we find Rohingya Crisis in Myanmar, territorial disputes in the South China Sea, tensions in the East China Sea, Islamist Militancy in Pakistan, Conflict Between India and Pakistan and of course the ongoing saber rattling between North Korea and the West. The long-standing unrest in the middle East continues unabated. There is instability in Lebanon and Egypt, and the Civil War in Libya. We see sporadic confrontations in the Cold War between the United States and Iran, the US war in Afghanistan and legacy of war in Iraq, War in Yemen and of course the almost eight decades old Israeli-Palestinian Conflict.

Closer to home, internal conflicts and narco-violence in Honduras, Mexico, Venezuela, and Colombia drive spending. Through Brazil alone, this accounts for about 51 percent of total military expenditures in South America. While we do not live with war here in the USA, the proxy wars in which America are embroiled contribute billions of dollars to the military industrial complex and to job creation. The tenor of the conflicts is varied, owing to all manner of ethnic and religious strife, some going back centuries. And these conflicts lead to instability and displacements of people.

The Impact of Forced Migration and the Need for Reconstruction

Today we find some 79.5 million individuals forcibly displaced worldwide as a result of persecution, conflict, violence or human rights violations of which 26.0 million are refugees – the highest ever seen; 45.7 million are internally displaced people; and 4.2 million are asylum-seekers. In the case of Syria alone, UN Economic and Social Commission for West Asia (ESCWA) estimates that it will take over $400 billion to reconstruct the country to its 2010 bricks and mortar condition. There is no estimate for what it will take to reweave the social fabric of a nation with 5 million refugees abroad and 6 million internally displaced, for the loss of social cohesion and social capital cannot be truly quantified. Wars, climate disasters and pandemics deeply affect our social psyche. Indeed, in the wake of all the disasters around the world, we have to question what "reconstruction" means. We cannot go back to what was. I would guestimate the cost of damage and subsequent rebuilding from all these skirmishes to be in the order of trillions of dollars. Who is going to pay for these reconstruction costs?

Why Reconstruct when We Can Terraform?

We are spending billions on the race for Space, in preparation for when we, having failed to secure Earth, will need to leave Earth, and create a home on other planets. We can only hope it does not devolve into yet another reason for conflict. We seem to be preparing for one or else why a Space Force? The US, EU, Russia India, Japan, China, and the UAE are vying to become Space powers. And we see a flurry of missions to the moon, Mars and asteroids, in various states of execution. The US Artemis program (which involves Europe) includes a series of manned deep-space missions and a Space Station that will orbit the moon later in the next decade. India has a lander mission to the moon. China plans to bring samples (2 kg) of lunar soil back to Earth. And the race goes on with all parties set to have basecamps on the moon by 2030.

Meanwhile Mars is on the mind. Europe EXOMARS project will send a robot rover to Mars to drill two meters below the surface to retrieve samples for study of past and possibly even present life on the planet. The US Mars 2020 rover will seek evidence that Mars was a place where water flowed, and life could have evolved. The highly, ambitious 2030 vision is that some of the rocks will be sealed and left in caches at designated sites on Mars to be collected by future joint European and US missions and brought back to Earth around 2030, while about 500g of rock will be returned to Earth for study in laboratories across the world. Not to be outdone, China and the UAE also plan to send probes to Mars. Meanwhile our study of how to mine asteroids is continuing. NASAs probe will sweep close to the asteroid Bennu's surface and extend a robot arm to collect samples and return to Earth sometime in 2023. Japan's near-Earth asteroid sample collection mission begun in 2018 and is due back to Earth before the end of 2020.

As if this were not enough, the billionaire boys' club quest for adventure has created a new twist in the race for Space. Their experiments have already reduced the cost of Space travel and building on the successful flight to the International Space Station in 2019, we expect that privately funded manned missions will become one of the main ways that astronauts (public and private) travel to and from the Space Station. Indeed, Space tourism plans are well on the way. Beyond the fear of privatization of Space, the existential threat that has some Space advocates worried is the talk of using nuclear fueled rockets. What if it were to explode and crash? Is there an APP for that? Not to worry. Constellations of satellites are being thrown up to guide the probes, as well as to blanket the world with the Internet and watch over us, so much so that astronomers fear that soon we won't be able to see the stars. The hopes for Space exploration and the capital invested in such dreams is rising.

Meanwhile Here on Earth, what Is Rising Is Inequality

As we say in the Caribbean, "tongue" has it to say that the race for Space constitutes yet another example of human folly. How is it that we can spend billions on one rocket but we cannot find funds to address hunger? How is it we can find ways to transport humans to Space and back, but we cannot find a solution to improve food distribution.

Is it not written in the good book that the poor shall always be among us? That said, it is still alarming to note that even in the time of COVID, the rich get richer, and the poor get poorer. As of 2020 there were over two thousand billionaires worldwide. These billionaires have a total net worth of $8 trillion. The world's 2,153 billionaires have more wealth than the 4.6 billion people who make up 60 percent of the planet's population. Oxfam's report, "Time to Care," calculates that the 22 richest men in the world have more wealth than all the women in Africa. Around the world, women and girls put in 12.5 billion hours of unpaid care work each, and every day – a contribution to the global economy of at least $10.8 trillion a year, more than three times the size of the global tech industry. Getting the richest one percent to pay just 0.5 percent extra tax on their wealth over the next ten years would equal the investment needed to create 117 million jobs in sectors such as elderly and childcare, education, and health. According to the global Fight Inequality Alliance, over 200 organizations around the world, while every government has pledged to reduce inequality within and between countries, in practice not much progress is happening. While global poverty rates have been cut by more than half since 2000, one in ten people in developing regions still lives on less than US$ 1.90 a day (over 730 million in 2015) –the internationally agreed poverty line, and millions of others live on slightly more than this daily amount. And the COVID-19 pandemic is increasing inequality as lower paid workers are more represented in the sectors that have suspended activities such as hotels, restaurants, and tourism services. A World Economic Forum survey of 37 countries indicates that 3 in 4 households have suffered declining income owing to the pandemic, with 82% of poorer households affected. Poverty entails more than the lack of income and productive resources to ensure sustainable livelihoods. People are struggling with hunger and malnutrition, limited access to education, health, water and sanitation and other basic services, social discrimination, and exclusion, as well as the lack of participation in decision-making.

The pandemic has highlighted the inequities in everything, especially in digital access, which now has seen increased calls to be treated as a human right. It has also highlighted inequalities in health. Despite factors like poor access to water and sanitation and medical infrastructure in developing countries, overall, the high inequality gap in worldwide healthcare distribution had been dropping as countries saw their life expectancy had been gradually improving. Then along came the COVID-19 pandemic (COVIDemic for short). No one has escaped the impact of the COVIDemic, and the fear of its cousins lurking in the heartland of the mostly unknown virosphere. Against the backdrop of ignominious calls to test the virus in Africa first, the unknown unknowns leave everyday conspiracy theorists with a lot of room for stoking fears about genocidal plans against Black peoples. And despite the hustle across the halls of science to engineer a successful search for effective tests, prophylactics, curatives, and vaccines, there are still more questions than answers. How will those vaccines reach the poorest nations? How will they be distributed with any kind of equity? How can a poor country get access to enough doses when nations like Canada and Switzerland are having issues? Especially given the unknown trajectory of the variants.

We Are a Living Mess. We Are Living in a Mesh.

Connecting the dots and gathering the threads of the stories brings us to a vexing array of challenges that might best be described as a hornets' nest. The consensus seems to be, "we cannot go back to business as usual." An interesting thing to note is that our language has begun to change. The typical call for a "War Against COVID" has not emerged as our lingua franca. It is as if we have loss the appetite for war, even righteous ones. Perhaps because the COVIDemic has been compounded by a global awakening or uprising to address racial and ethnic discrimination. The genie of discontent cannot easily be stuffed back into its bottle. Not for nothing did thousands take to the streets in Europe and Asia in solidarity with George Floyd whose name now signifies a general resentment against the system. Be it against the foot of steel-toe booted police or what I call the Gross Deprivation Production (the real GDP) demanded by the status quo, the demands being made in the streets are for change. Caretakers of our plural society seem to have little to no desire to reawake many of our now comatose economic and social systems. There is the sense that there is a real opportunity for us to cross the chasms from the future we wanted which seemed out of reach – to the future we can now have if we work for it.

What is needed is for us to give voice to what is being left out of our public conversations. There are many seeds of change and bright spots of hope in the terrain of the emerging future. Even those who trade in the seductive voice of fear, all the better to boost ratings and clicks, seem open to change. There is an admission that the time has come for a reboot. For the reality is we are all in this together. As the saying goes "There is no Planet B." Really. The fate of Generation Z who will be 100 years young at the turn of the twenty-second century is at stake. A just future that allows for their future wellbeing requires us to ensure we stop depleting Pacha Mama's resources faster than she can replenish them. As we seek to approach Homo sapiens deus in our technological might, surely, we can design means to ensure our survival on Earth.

The gospel of growth at all costs, which contributed to the enslavement of millions of people of African descent to economic man, has brought us to this very bitter-sweet state. For we have come to realize that this "good" life in the fast lane with all its joys and benefits is also killing us. The hunt for money and more money holds out false hope, for money as we know it may be on the way out. Experts predict that by 2050 cash will be history; your wallet will only be a card or some app in your personal digital assistant that provides you with virtual currency. The entire monetary system is about to go through changes. It was one thing to talk about crypto currency when it was for the fringe elements. It is another when Facebook, with over one billion daily users, talks about launching its own cryptocurrency. The announcement set off shock waves. What will become of national central banks? Good question. The future of money is by no means certain, and even while it might remain true that money makes the world go round, it does not necessarily make you happier. Many of the happiest countries in the world are the Scandinavian countries, but Colombia and Jamaica do well on the list, and they certainly are not among the wealthiest in the world. Maybe it is time to look at the Gross National Happiness (GNH) as a global metric that can help lead us to a regenerative economy. How do we better value the future so that we can ensure our flourishing?

Where Do We Go from Here?

These are perilous times. Around the world, freedom, civility, and truth are threatened. The choices we make now will define our future for generations to come. As an African friend of mine puts it, "When we find ourselves standing at the edge of a cliff, a wise person recognizes that a progressive move is to step back." In the spirit of Sankofa, the Akan people's proverb which states "it is alright to go back and fetch what was left behind," we may need to return to humility and borrow from the wisdom of the indigenous peoples, much that we have in our arrogance defined as "backwards," to find our way forward to a better place. The question then becomes where? Where is Wakanda?

This lockdown has not meant that we are locked up or locked in or locked away from our various Tribes and clans which see the world through the prisms of our own reality, often to the detriment of us being able to see and hear through the eyes of the other. There are as many movements as there are challenges, and even within each movement there are various strains that signify various responses to the ever-changing landscape. New movements are forever forming, storming and norming, and the revolutions will be televised, and arrive live on social media. We are in a time where the rise of individual power has made it possible for a few people to effect change. The Arab Spring, the Hong Kong protests, the Children's Climate Fridays for the Future Movement, Black Lives Matter have all brought into sharper focus the danger ahead. The climate change clan of the Caretaker Tribe have put about the story that Mother Nature or Pacha Mama shut us down so she could breathe. The political Leader Tribe and the private-sector Merchant Tribe are looking for ways to build back better. The Medusas of media and entertainment have ensured that via the 24-hour entertainment news cycle the images of a world at risk are seared into our subconscious.

What remains is for us to connect the dots, and to find a way to truly connect. Among the Zulu people, the greeting ritual "Sawubona" (meaning "I see you. I value you. I respect you") to which the response "Shikoba" comes (meaning "I exist for you") offers food for thought. How might we create a mindset that allows us to connect and find ways to weave the different strands of thought of our various clans and Tribes from the environmental movement to the women's movement, prison reform, antiracism, antifood waste, save the ocean, save the apes, anti-AI, anti-nuclear, anti-human-trafficking movements and more. All these clans in the plural tribe have a role in our shared story. All the Tribes have a role in co-creating our shared futures on our shared planet.

What I Believe

All the doom and gloom statistics have not rubbed the shine off my optimism. I claim an opportunity hidden in the COVIDemic. Some countries may be doing much better than others in terms of deaths and other health statistics, but our global economy is so intertwined that no country will escape without a swipe. It is mindboggling to people around the world that travelers from the USA are mostly unwelcome or banned. This is a total shift of consciousness. This shift creates an opening. This is what is called for: a shift in global consciousness. The COVIDemic provides us the opportunity to have more everyday people to make the shift from global consumer to global citizen.

We have the opportunity to reimagine our roles on the stage of life, as we write the story of human history. All of us will have to re-think and re-member the future we want in the post-COVID New Normal. We all need to ask ourselves the question: What might this new normal be for our personal lives, the future of the communities in which we live, work, and play and do business? Our Leaders in governments of nation-states, cities, or towns all must rethink what should be the role of the government. Our Merchants, those in the private sector, all will need to rethink their role. Our Educators will need to reimagine the role of the academy in education and training of humans for the new world. The Caretakers in our plural civil society — from the faith community to the professional associations, from grassroots rural women's clubs to the NGOs with UN recognition status, from community development organizations to international service organizations like Rotary and the Boy Scouts — will all need to revise their vision, mission and purpose to make the pivot necessary to help us thrive. And not to be left out, the Talebearers in the field of media and entertainment will need to reform what they believe to be true of their role and recognize that they too are responsible for the future we are creating.

Looking at this global pandemic through the eyes of the long view, we can choose to see, instead of a nuisance or a stagnation, a welcome pause that provides for a period of gestation. We have the time to grow and birth and midwife new ways of being. We can now choose to multiply and bring to scale the bright spots of hope and the seeds of change that have been demonstrating how it might be possible to live within our boundaries and reset the trajectory of human endeavor.

The differences we see and use as dividing lines can be recast as threads in our collective human story's tapestry. Whether we are talking about social issues, technological issues, environmental issues, economic issues, or political issues, these are all our shared issues, our shared stories. *Now* we get to see *who* we truly are. As they say in the church "sometimes we need a setback, so we can have a setup for a comeback."

In the COVID-induced global quarantine even as we are spatially distanced, we need to sing a requiem for the future lost as we reimagine another way onward. We cannot afford to wait and see what might emerge unattended. As Buckminster Fuller said, we are all crew on spaceship Earth. And there are no passengers. Even though it seems like chaos we have the power to be the change. We might heed the words of science fiction writer Octavia E. Butler in the *Book of the Living,* which calls on us to "Shape Chaos. Act. Alter the speed or the direction of Change. Vary the scope of Change. Recombine the seeds of Change. Transmute the impact of Change. Seize Change. Use it. Adapt and grow." We need a new gospel to be sent forth into the world to multiply as quickly as possible. Bob Marley's "One Love" as the song of the twentieth century, known to millions of people the world over, might be the global non-sectarian anthem we need. But, before we can sing a new gospel, we must accept the death of that vision of the future lost which no longer serves us. Only then can we set off to the flourishing future the way we want. But wait. What is the future we want? Are we all agreed that we want to save our Planet Earth? This book is about how we weave the tapestry of lives and futures by the questions that we use to explore, envision, edify and experience our world and the stories we tell ourselves.

Day Two
The Year 2100
Anansi Arrives in Time to Catch the Headline News for
UN Human Rights Day

December 10, 2100… International Human Rights Day
The Global Gleaner News
Alix Inder Wundelund, Good News Correspondent

One hundred and fifty centenarians, who were founding members of the youth arm of the Ubuntu Alliance formed in the wake of the COVID-19 pandemic to accelerate achievement of the UN Agenda 2030, back in 2020 gathered to celebrate the Centennial Covenant in Addis Ababa at the Headquarters of the African Union. Coming from 50 countries around the world, all except 20 will appear in situ. The other twenty members of the "Ubuntu Avengers" as they called themselves in a parody of the Marvel comics' super-heroes will attend via the holotram, the latest transmission medium taking the world by storm. These days turning 100 is not surprising, what with nanotechnology making human part replacements and human AI brain interface making aging diseases like arthritic hips and dementia a thing of the past. The decision to change the global standard of Gross National Product to Gross National Wellbeing in 2030 made a huge difference in ensuring human flourishing took center stage as a feature of eudemonic policy activism. As members of the Talebearer Clan of the Ubuntu Alliance, they had executed a series of highly, successful transmedia storytelling projects to cultivate a mindset shift to a regenerative economy or "Lifesaver Economics" principles in the relay to achievement of the Sustainable Development Goals, (UN Agenda 2030). Several blockbuster films and games created from 2020 through to 2040 had not only created jobs and built a new cooperative economy but had resulted in a following of over two billion people combined across all their platforms by 2045. This following was channeled into political credits resulting in significant members of the

Ubuntu Alliance being elected at local levels in countries around the world, who collectively were responsible for securing Future Wellbeing Acts in almost 100 countries by 2050 and the Twenty-First-Century Covenant. Today they commemorate the fiftieth anniversary of the Covenant and its achievements which included a 10 billion population cap, as well as the Just Space Economy Agreements that ensured the rights to Space for all.

The Moon Settlements established in 2050 have become truly inclusive.

The formative decades of the 2020s and 2030s of the Ubuntu Alliance read like the pages of a high escapade thriller, but their fortitude and wisdom was forged from living through the ABC (Australia, Brazil, California) wildfires, the Friday Climate Movements, the refugee camps and the mass shootings in schools across America. For the founding flock, the motto "People in Power" and their hacktivist skills armed them with tools to survive the many threats to decimate the movement. True, it was too late for the many animals and species that had gone extinct, and even today there are fears that the emperor penguins may not make it because of the loss of sea ice and depletion of krill in Antarctica. Since 2070, nearly 200 million people have had to be resettled in seasteads (both ships and islands) around the world as it was more effective to let go of cites like Miami, Shanghai, Lagos, Sydney, and Venice where repeated flooding made the sea walls ineffective.

But, it could be a lot worse, for we succeeded in keeping the temperature rise just below 1.7 degrees by 2050. Tonight's concert will feature holographic performances of one hundred global musical icons over the past century simulcast from the African World Heritage Museum in Accra, the Planetary Futures Museum in Sydney and the Oceanic Heritage Museum in Kingston, and close with "One Love" global chorus in the Holo amphitheater with over 1 million people from every corner of the world participating. Finally, three one-hundred-year time capsules set to be opened in the year 2200 will be buried on the Earth, Moon and on Mars. SMART Futures await. Onward!

Chapter 2

What Is the Future We Want?

We are in a very pregnant pause. As we think about our future as a largely urban global society, we ask, "how will we live, work, play in a new hypervigilant world?" In the future we want, post-COVID New Normal emerges as the best of who we can be. We ask the questions: What does it mean to be a smart community? What does it mean to be a just society? What does it mean to be a sustainable, thriving, flourishing society? In this future, we have gone beyond the allure of the smartphones and smart cars, smart homes, smart cities and smart cities and communities, to designing a smart society. We have secured smart futures.

This pause has gifted us an opportunity to think anew. We have had to confront not just the abstract "issues of global health and security" but also our personal health and wellbeing. We have had to confront the legacy of the stories we have been telling about race because of a global eruption of rage, lit by the smartphone images of police brutality and the haunting sound of a man's last words, "I can't breathe." So how do we come to a truly shared vision that sees beyond and around this hornets' nest to the future we want? It's going to take a different kind of leadership, or stewardship, to be able to bring all the different Tribes and clans to this state of being. We need to answer two questions that come from popular songs. The first is the underlying assumption that we can "get it if we really want it." Is that really true? And if so, is it sustainable? The second question to address is when we hold hands and sing "We are the World," who exactly is we? Of primary importance is that we need to understand how we got here, our history and the myths that feed our belief before we can look at our decision-making in a SMART way. As of 2020, there are 7.8 billion people in the world. Who are *WE*? For our purposes I am going to define us, this human family, according to the subsystems or Tribes that can be used to define global governance rules working on one thing or another.

WE are, some of us, in the public sector – I will call the Leader Tribe. At the global level this tribe is led by the United Nations and its alphabet soup group of agencies from FAO to UNOOSA to WHO, WTO and all the others outside of this Clan that ascribe and prescribe the various rulebooks by which we live our lives, from the smallest hamlet to the largest city in the world.

WE are, some of us, in the private sector – I will call the Merchant Tribe – corralled into some semblance of order by various global, national, state and local organizations such as the World Chemical Energy Council, World Energy Council or World Shipping Council.

Some of us are educators – I call the Mentor Tribe – who dwell in the academic sphere and schools, but also work as coaches, trainers, webinar facilitators, guides. They teach us all the capabilities we will need for the new world.

Some of us are in the media and entertainment sector–I will call the Talebearer Tribe. You know who they are. They keep us enthralled by the neck of our lizard brains in a 24-hour news cycle of mostly bad news brain candy.

And finally, *WE* are some of us, in the plural sector–I will call the Caretaker Tribe. The plural sector is about communities as opposed to the private sector which is about the market and the public sector which is about government. This tribe includes all variants of civil organizations big and small, global to local, from the International Confederation of Labor Unions to World Parliament of Religions to Amnesty International to Ocean Conservancy to Rotary International and the Girl Scouts. All of us, billions, live our lives as members of two or more Tribes and clans at the same time. We exist as a hive, a complex meshwork of relationships and rules. We are at once a planetary species, a global society, and local communities. It will take all of us working together in SMART ways to cultivate the paradigm shift we need to save ourselves and our planet.

Planetary Species History

Our most recent declaration on a shared vision of our common global good was enshrined in the United Nations Agenda defined in 2015, in which 191 nations of the world agreed it was in our collective best interest to agree on 17 Sustainable Development Goals with 169 targets to be achieved by the year 2030. Before we detail the vision, it is worthwhile pausing to reflect on how we came to this pass.

Most of us would agree that the notion of ourselves as a planetary species first took hold of our imaginations when we first saw ourselves as a blue marble floating in the dark void of Space. This was 1969. The Cold War was at a high. But for this moment, with millions of eyes glued to the television which was now available across much of the world's capital cities even on small islands like Jamaica, much of the world was of one accord. "The world would never be the same."

The actual history of the globalization of our economy and our governance architecture is a complex map (mesh) of conferences and treaties and wars and incidents that would take books to recount. A few highlights are useful for our purposes. In looking at the future we want to co-create it is important to look at how we got here – not only on the litany of what happened in terms of the material reality of recorded history and its observed artifacts, which in many instances is the story of those who won the war. We must also reflect on the causes – the economic, cultural, political factors – that helped to create the reality we live with today. In addition, we need to explore the discourse that legitimizes and supports the institutional structure of how we live our lives with such deep inequality around the world between and within countries. Once we grapple with these structures, we can excavate the metaphors and myths that underlie the psychological and mental foundations of group cosmologies of haste and waste.

We came to this pass as a result of three ships that went sailing westward from Europe to find new trade routes to the East back around 1492. For me, this is the turning point in human history, for it set into motion the birth of the Trans-Atlantic Slave Trade in Africans from the 1500s to the 1800s, which is the foundation cornerstone of the market capitalist system which now dominates our world economy. Moreover, this system gave birth to the pernicious meme of white superiority and the prevailing notion of a racial order in which as the 1947 Big Bill Broozy blues protest song lamented, "If you're white you should be alright, if you're brown stick around, if you're black get back." Understanding this as a metaphor and myth that underlies much of the psychological conflict that bubbles under the surface of our global dealings is vital. Understanding this meme is also important, because when we talk about inequality and inequity, we forget that much of the world order we have today is a consequence of centuries of race-based legal discrimination. So, as we think about making a shift to achieving global sustainability, we need to be much more clear-eyed about analyzing the problems we are trying to solve. There is a reason why skin bleaching cream sales topped US$8 billion across the world in 2020 from Asia to Africa. We need to remember that. We cannot discuss the future we want without being ready to examine the cornerstones of the paradigms on which we have built the houses in which we now live.

Sankofa! Let me go back and fetch what we might have forgotten. This global trade in Africans was the bedrock of the wealth created in and for Europe. Along the way over-tired from ongoing wars such as the Thirty Years' War – a series of wars in Central Europe between 1618 and 1648 which started as a war between various Protestant and Catholic states in the fragmented Holy Roman Empire; and the Eighty Years' War, or Dutch War of Independence (1568–1648), in 1648, they signed a series of treaties come to be known as the Peace of Westphalia. The Peace of Westphalia established the precedent of peace reached by diplomatic congress and a new system of political order in Europe based upon the concept of co-existing sovereign states. The Westphalian principle of the recognition of another state's sovereignty and right to decide its own fate rests at the foundations of international law today.

If only those principles had carried over to the European colonization of Asia and Africa in the nineteenth century and the two global wars in the twentieth century. Indeed, when the powers of the day convened the African Conference in Berlin, on a November day in 1884, representatives of every country in Europe, except for Switzerland, showed up and spent some 104 days (counting in the holiday break) to hammer out agreements that carved out control of Africa, not one African was invited to participate in the conversation. This confab set down another foundation stone in our global governance system and paved the way for the evolution of colonialism so that at the end of World War I, which lasted from 1914 to 1918, ended when the League of Nations was formed in 1919 (1920) to maintain world peace, almost all the countries in Africa and Asia were still colonies or protectorates of the powers in Europe. This war and treaty which considered issues like the arms trade and prisoners of war and minorities in Europe was a big step towards our view of ourselves as one world. The advent of the Spanish flu pandemic (1918 to early 1920) in which millions of people died was also a game changer.

Another major turning point to global mindset was the advent of the scientific marvels like the telegraph. We could also mark the formation of the International Telecommunications Union, which was the first international organization back in 1865, setting out rules for the new technology of the telegraph. This was our first tech-related agreement. The Paris Exposition of 1900 introduced ideas that would shape the twentieth century. The world's fair visited by over fifty million visitors featured flying machines, diesel engines, talking films, escalators, and the first magnetic audio recorder, called the telegraphone. Zounds! No wonder Paris became a city of lights! There was also the Olympics games which was restarted in Greece in 1896 with 241 participants from 13 nations to over 10,000 people from over 200 nations and territories. Another phenomenon that has helped people think of themselves as part of a global community is the quadrennial frenzy known as World Cup Football. The real football – played with the foot – put on by International Football Federation best known by its French acronym as (FIFA). FIFA was founded in 1904 with nine member countries – mostly from Europe. Today FIFA has 209 members. It is hard to claim we are not part of a global community when 3.5 billion pairs of eyes are glued to screens and the football mad world slows down to a crawl, the night of FIFA World Cup finals. If only the opening of the United Nations General Assembly could attract 10 percent of that, we would be so lucky. FIFA should be seen as a proxy for a global consciousness, a seed for global awareness of our interdependence. It has had more impact in keeping hope of peace alive than the United Nations and the Bretton Woods Institutions – the World Bank and the IMF combined.

However, in the last 75 years, since the formation of the United Nations, we have seen the outgrowth of scores, if not hundreds, of global organizations that form the global architecture – that is, functional agencies that deal with issues from health to population, to human rights, to refugees, to energy, to war, to trade, to food to economics and more. For every issue that plagues humanity, there is an agency, or an office, or an institution at the global level that is designing the rulebook that attempts to set guidelines on how we share this planet. We may not be perfect, but we could congratulate ourselves a little for the fact that we are trying.

The Universal Declaration of Human Rights that was drafted by the United Nations General Assembly on December 10, 1948, created a new standard on the fundamental rights of human beings. This declaration is the basis on which a lot of progress has been made in terms of rule of law and more recently what is called the right to development. The right to development includes but is not limited to the rights to food, education, work, and fair pay. However, because it was placed in an economic framework only, we have the systems we have today. These systems are based on the dominant Judeo-Christian view of the world as filtered through an economic lens.

The Turning Point

The right to development was placed in an economic framework that does not value human development and human rights and does not truly improve the wellbeing of every member of society. In the 1990s Nobel Prize for Economics winner Amartya Sen developed a whole new theory to help address this shortcoming. He put forth the capability of approach to development and poverty and put on the map the concept of development, not being just about the consumption of goods, and people as human resources. He called into question the notion of the primacy of the paradigm of the economic value of humanity, which was based on the belief that people are more developed if they consume more.

This was a turning point in my thinking because as an agent of the development assistance industry, I found myself at odds with the gospel of development I was told to preach. I can remember a time growing up in Jamaica when we did not have a lot, but our quality of life was better. None of our houses had burglar bars. We did not know what it was to have somebody steal something in our neighborhood. And we were able to walk the streets at night without streetlights at the time back and forth, without a problem. Children could play outside with nobody fearful that they would be kidnapped or taken away by a random person. What have we been developed into?

When Amartya Sen said, "The primary focus of development should be the focus of people as human beings, not the expansion of the economy," it was as if a light bulb was turned on. Sen's capability approach really helped us to understand development differently, but his ideas did not gain enough momentum or get rooted deep enough to point us away from the thrall of the Gross Domestic Product. So, even though we have other metrics like the Human Development Index (HDI) and the Wellbeing Index, the GDP is still the thing to toast. Governments and leaders boast about GDP not their HDI. The get high on growth, not on wealth and income distribution.

In 1970, we celebrated the first Earth Day which set the popularization of the global environmental movement into motion. The 1980s to 1990s brought several global confabulations that helped shift social norms. We had the Beijing Conference on Women, which gave voice and agency to millions of movements around the world. We had a Quincentennial of the arrival of Columbus in the Americas, and the Declaration of Indigenous Peoples which gave visibility to their ancient cosmologies and helped more of us to understand other worldviews – the Inuit, Maya, Maori, Navajo, Puja and Wiradjuri people – such as "the Earth does not belong to humans, rather humans belong to the Earth." These ideas complemented and broadened and deepened the environmental consciousness and paved the way for the climate movements to take off. And thus, the noosphere began to speak of sustainable development.

Conferencing for the Future

At the beginning of the twenty-first century, the UN hosted

the third World Conference on Racism, Racial Discrimination and Xenophobia (UNWCAR) in Durban, South Africa. This was yet another critical turning point in the conversation on the global nature of colonialism and its constructs which had embedded memes of "a natural hierarchy of racial order" around the world. The UNWCAR Durban Conference (which I was a party to drafting language for) among other things, called for changing the rules and regulations and practices in the international financial institutions as well as the transnational corporations. The visions embodied by the Plan of Action are still on the horizon.

There have been many global conferences other than the ones I have highlighted. Conferences to address biodiversity targets, renewable energy, water, good, environment, the ocean, you name it there has been a conference for it. We humans excel at conferencing. It is a global multibillion-dollar industry. Whole city blocks-sized convention centers have been built as shrines to our conferencing with the requisite hotels and the like providing thousands of jobs. You might think all this talking is a waste. But I say, "better $millions in conferencing than $billions in wars."

A big turning point for global governance systems was the millennial development goals launched in the year 2000. The turn of the century was very important psychologically.

The turn of the century, the year 2000, was a very heady time and the development assistance community clan, all the agencies – multilaterals such as the World Bank, African Development Bank, Asian Development Bank, Inter-American Development Bank, Islamic Development Bank; and bi-laterals like US Agency for international Development, the Japanese International Cooperation Agency, the British Department for International Development, the Swedish, the Norwegian, Canadian — every single agency from any country went through a period of reflection. The words "donor fatigue" were being thrown about.

And, at the same time, there was rising the voice of the "Fifty Years Is Enough" movement calling for Debt Relief and Jubilee. The sentiment on the one hand was "We've been spending all this money doing development and we're not seeing a return on investment. It is enough." The sentiment on the other hand was "You've been lending all this money to poor countries, causing them to rack up insurmountable debts that do not get at the problem caused by your centuries of exploitation. Fifty years is enough. Really." Together these arguments created fertile ground for the establishment of a new idea. What if we had goals that we all agreed on were important to making the difference we say we want to see? The Millennium Development Goals (MDGs)set in 2020, were a milestone accomplishment. It was the first time there was an attempt to put a goal and targets on what we as a global polity were trying to achieve. And it was really a huge change in the way the development community saw themselves and their work.

The MDGs had eight goals and 60 indicators to measure progress on things like eradicating extreme poverty and hunger, achieving universal primary education, promoting gender equality and empowering women, reducing child mortality, improving maternal health, combating HIV/AIDS, Malaria and other diseases, ensure an environmental sustainability, and developing a global partnership for development. As someone who was actively agitating for racial equity in the development assistance industry at the time, I saw the MDGs as a huge opportunity. I was able to use the goals to push the agenda for development with equity and make the argument for metrics that measured the economic impact of racial discrimination in Latin America, to push the issue for improving the collection of racial statistics in the censuses across Latin America. Mind you, it was a lonely road, there were not many takers, but it certainly gave me a little cover for what many people saw as my outlaw focus on racial discrimination. At that point in the global economic discourse, as defined by the Washington Consensus, to use the words racism or ethnic discrimination in polite company was considered bad form at best, and heresy at worse. Did the MDGs achieve its promise? Not precisely. It was a challenge to get people to buy into the idea of goal-based plans. It was a challenge to make the targets and indicators sexy, to make them mean something to stakeholders. But we did see evidence of progress made in terms of poverty reduction, primary education, girls' education, and health and disease outcomes, and improving access to water. The MDGs helped to create a new way of speaking to global development challenges and paved the way for corporate actors like the Gates Foundation to join a Compact. The MDGs helped NGOs to focus and to organize differently. The MDGs were a good building block for what is now in our global sights – the Sustainable Development Goals. It was a solid attempt at addressing the future from the perspective of shared power and shared responsibility. The MDGs were the first time we had a shared benchmark for what we wanted to create as a global good. But it was hampered by its failure to catch on with the millions of global citizens it needed to press into service. And as for the marketing? What does "halve poverty by 50 percent" mean to the average person? Nada. Nothing. Zilch.

Back to 2015 and Shared Visions of Agenda 2030 and Beyond

Now that we see how we got to where we are, for many of the Tribes, we can look at the shared visions of the future and understand where we see ourselves going. UN Agenda 2030, the Sustainable Development Goals (SDGs) which were launched in 2015, is a riff off the MDGs. It was an arduous negotiation between governments and civil society. Because, of course, everybody wanted their issue in there. And, yet people still complain that there's too much in the goals. The goals range from zero poverty; to ending hunger; good health and wellbeing; education; gender equality; clean water and sanitation; affordable and clean energy; decent work and economic growth; industry, innovation, and infrastructure; reduced inequality; sustainable cities and communities; responsible consumption and production; climate action; life below water; life on land; peace and justice strong institutions, and partnerships to achieve the goals. They cover everything it would seem except for information communications technologies (ICTs) and Space.

The SDGs are a shared vision about the future we want, because the goals are intended to be relevant for every country not just developing countries. Countries are supposed to hand in report cards. Corporate actors who have signed compacts are supposed to show how they have contributed in their annual reports and civil society actors are urged to become multipliers. There is significant hustle and bustle with civil society organizations jostling to get picked to present in the NGO Action Zone where ostensibly we are supposed to share our ideas and network and learn from each other. It is truly a major experiment in global social engineering.

The issue with the SDGs that has had many people dubious is, whether countries and parties would have the discipline to do what is needed to meet the goals from day one. And now with COVID, the thinking is that it will be impossible to advance the SDGs for years – given the global economic setback. Even in countries where the pandemic has not had undue impact on people's physical health, it has undone many economic gains in countries – all over. Indeed, the handling of the COVID-19 pandemic in Europe and the US has made it clear that contrary to popular opinion, the health care systems in many WEIRD countries are challenged by disparities and inequality. Still the SDGs are a concrete vision that all nations share and that we have pledged to address.

A rethinking of how we talk about economics has led to

a new meme called donut economics so-called because the infographic is drawn as two circles with a hole in the middle. Given the ambitions and hope in the ring, with all respect to the "visioneur" economist Kate Raworth, I would rather call it "Lifesaver Economics." Re-designing the operating procedure for global systems to operate on the principles of Lifesaver Economics would make a major difference in our relay to the next milestone in global survival stakes, 2050.

Climate

The Kyoto Protocol was adopted in 1997, represented the first time that nations agreed to legally mandated, country-specific emissions reduction targets. The protocol, which went into effect in 2005, set binding emissions reduction targets for developed countries only, on the premise that they were responsible for most of the Earth's high levels of greenhouse gas emissions. The United States signed the agreement but never ratified because China and India, the other two big polluters, were not included. Without the participation of those three countries, the treaty's effectiveness was limited.

In 2012, the plans were made to create a new, comprehensive climate treaty by 2015 that would require all big emitters not included in the Kyoto Protocol – such as China, India, and the United States – to reduce their greenhouse gas emissions. The new treaty – called the Paris Agreement – was to fully replace the Kyoto Protocol by 2020. However, the Paris accord after much lobbying by the small island developing states went into effect in 2016. The Paris Accord for the first time brought all nations into a common cause to undertake ambitious efforts to combat climate change and adapt to its effects, with enhanced support to assist developing countries to do so. As a shared vision for the future we want, it was to chart a new course in global gamesmanship. Specifically, the central aim of the Paris Agreement, adopted by 196 parties in December 2015, was to pursue efforts to limit the temperature increase to 1.5 degrees Celsius and keep global temperature rise to well below 2 degrees Celsius above pre-industrial levels.

Additionally, the agreement aimed to strengthen the ability of countries to deal with the impacts of climate change. To reach these ambitious goals, appropriate financial flows, a new technology framework and an enhanced capacity building framework will be put in place, thus supporting action by developing countries and the most vulnerable countries, in line with their own national objectives. The Agreement called for enhanced transparency of action – nationally determined contributions (NDCs) and support through a more robust transparency framework for reporting regularly and doing global stocktaking every 5 years to assess the collective progress and to inform further actions.

When the US federal government pulled America out of the Paris agreement on November 4, 2020, it really was as a result of misinformation. First of all, there was the story that the Paris agreement would hurt the US economy – as it would cost the US economy millions of dollars, and thousands of jobs, and that would make us less competitive against China and India. Studies have shown that this statement was not, and is not, true. Thankfully, many cities and counties in America decided to agree to set targets at the local level. They see what is happening in Louisiana islands in the low country, under water with people losing their land, and having to move into the city for work and for life. They see the wildfires and tornadoes. They see what is happening in Europe and so they have envisioned a Clean Power Plan, or the Green New Deal, or a local response. The reality is that the scientific community has warned that we could cross the 1.5 degree threshold as early as 2025, even if global emissions were to be suddenly reduced to desired targets, because of what is already in the system. While the US has rejoined the Paris Agreement as of February 21, 2021, many here in the US still dither about a shared vision of climate limits, while around the rest of the world, most are rolling up their sleeves and asking what can we do? A survey done by Pew Research Trust shows that there's agreement globally that people blame global warming on human activity, and people saying that there's an urgent need for a collective approach from private, public, and plural societies to advance these agendas.

The Talebearers

There is a special role for media and entertainment or the Talebearer Tribe as I call them. Just think, there are close to 5 billion mobile phones, and indeed, the smartphone is the greatest democratization vehicle that we do have, because it can deliver news from anywhere at any time — 24 hours, 7 days a week, 365 days per year. So, within minutes, the tweet of the moment can morph into a global meme. This creates many possibilities for creating shared ideas, shared values, and shared vision on life after COVID.

We live in a very, complex system of systems. And the future we want as individuals should coalesce around the wounds in the body of Earth, whether you are working on food security, or environmental justice, or climate change. All our futures converge to create the mesh work that is the Earth system in which we live, and to which we belong. Agenda 2030 with its 17 goals and 169 targets is a good milestone on the way to achieving sustainability. The population will be close to 8.3 billion in the year 2030. In 2040, the population will be 9 billion and water could become a huge problem. In 2050, our current tag year for any major infrastructure investment made such as a road, a bridge, a housing complex, power plants, and the start of climate apocalypse if we don't turn around, the population is expected to be 9.7 billion. Meanwhile, 2030 is lurking in the hallways waiting to rush in. Can you imagine 2030? Can you imagine meeting the SDGs? What stands in our way? Is it a lack of faith in this vision of the future? What if there were a way to get people believing in their inevitability? What if we could make a paradigm shift to a SMART Future?

Day Three
The Year 2070
Anansi Drops Down on Earth Day Just in Time to Sit in
on the Earth Day Centennial Awards

Speech of the Chair of Just Space Futures Alliance at the Earth Day Centennial Awards

April 24, 2070

Fellow Humans. Friends All. Thank you for the accolades you have placed on me. I accept on behalf of my clan and crew, some of whom joined with me to establish the Just Space Futures Alliance and launched the SPACE GOODWILL GAMES almost fifty years ago. As some of you know, the Space Goodwill Games were a vision of my Mentor, who we knew and loved as Alpha Xaymacaluna. When the proposal to organize a SPACE GOODWILL GAMES was first made in 2022 at a meeting of UNOOSA, none of us knew how it would come to pass. Indeed, we were called delusional. Our remit as the Just Space Futures Alliance more popularly known as the UPSTARTS (short for the United Planetary Society to Assure Rights to Space) was simply to ensure that none of humanity was left behind. When we began our work, the Space economy was largely the purview of private enterprises and wealthy individuals. Today, Space travel is relatively affordable and Space tourism has gained traction. Here on Lunarville Sol, which we established as the first cooperatively funded lunar base back in 2040, we have been expanding our dream to live as if humanity matters. Our village now houses a total of 200 people of whom 50 are short-term tourists. In addition to room for tourists, we have added new scientific modules with greenhouses, ice harvesting stations for water, and solar arrays built from lunar regolith. What we do here is for all humanity.

We understand that in order to maintain our way of life and the Universe which sustains us, we must be ever vigilant to the first law

of ecology. There is no place such as away. We are all connected. What we do here on the Moon is connected to what you do on Earth.

Asteroid mining aspirations and technology is evolving, with major firms competing in research and development in the race to spare Pacha Mama further insult. Here in Lunarville Sol some are doing research on how we might mine main belt asteroids to recover metals and minerals we will need to fuel our interplanetary family, so that we might keep our land for ensuring food and water systems we have developed. Our human family of 10 billion demands that we continue to do better to become better at ensuring we maintain what we have achieved since 2030 including access to health and education for all.

We can continue to be proud that the ozone layer has fully recovered, and we have staved off desertification. We can continue to learn better how to cooperate with the natural world to reduce the likelihood and impact of future pandemics. We must continue to ensure that we keep our temperature rise under 2 °C. We must continue to be vigilant and ensure we do not make technology our God. Technology will not save us, for as we see despite recent advances in energy, food production and healthcare technology, we are still grappling with the human challenge, life within the boundaries of the "LifeSaver" Ubuntu Agreements. The price for our continued wellbeing is eternal vigilance. I accept this Award as Guardian of the Galaxy – this name is meaningful to me. I used to love those comic books as a child. I accept this Award as I accept that our work is never ending. Our "global commons" of instantly shared knowledge and freely available resources from our global meshwork, gives us all we need to protect our freedoms and our futures. Whether we are living in old cities or new cities, big nations or micro-nations, in cavesteads, floating islands or seasteads, on Earth or on the Moon and Mars colonies, we are all connected. While we search for life among the stars, let us continue to preserve and protect our Mother Earth. Onwards! Ubuntu!

Chapter 3

What Is Standing in Our Way?

If we know where we're coming from, and we know where we want to go, what is standing in our way? We have been to the moon and are planning to go back. We have built a probe capable of traveling at over 430,000 mph to the sun. Surely, we can find a way to feed the hungry and care for the sick? The reality is that sustainability, and the march to achieving it, requires a meshwork of policies, programs or projects. And this approach means collaborating as opposed to coexisting as silos of peoples, organizations and institutional arrangements.

Insufficient Recognition of Interconnectedness

It is common to see the challenges to achieving sustainability and sustainable development as a failure in political will and governance structures. We created carrot sticks to induce change, but we have no bamboo sticks with which to enforce infractions. We have also inherited global rulebooks which have largely favored the power status quo. And power does not cede itself without cause. Taking the issue of energy, for example, even though we know in theory that we should transition to green energy much faster than we are doing, we tinker around on the edges. Even as oil companies claim they are leading the move to renewable energy, they are busily drilling for oil in some of the most fragile places like the Arctic, and the Caribbean Sea. The latter issue brings up the conundrum that smaller nations like Guyana and Suriname face which is how to balance the possibility of oil wealth against rising sea levels that will decimate their own coastlines. And God forbid there is an oil spill. The sea has no borders. Not to mention no one knows the long-term impact or blowback from drilling holes all over the ocean floor. Therein lies another failure.

Failure to see second and third order impacts is another reason we have not created a sustainable future for ourselves. Would that we had compound eyes like a dragonfly that can see almost 360 degrees at the same time and see the whole spectrum of light. Our view is too limited. We are hampered by shortsightedness, quite often congenital. By and large, our governance architecture and the way we are educated and trained and organized are not able to deal with the reality that everything is everything. We are not trained to deal with systems and systems of systems challenges. The SDGs lay out 17 goals and 169 targets, but we have not described the intersectionality between them, in large part because we can't. At least not in the usual quantitative way we look at problem-solving. We know we can't eradicate poverty in all its dimensions and forms without combatting inequality within and among countries. We know we cannot address health care without addressing access to water and sanitation and education and access to nutritious food, which takes us back to poverty which redounds to inequality. There is no clear border or boundary to where one challenge ends and another begins. However, our policies and programs and projects tend to be designed as if there are clear boundaries. We are not thinking as if we understand we need SMART solutions.

Our public sector (Leader Tribe) is designed to operate in silos – global, national, local are all structured along sector lines. At the global level, we find an alphabet soup of organizations from World Trade to UN Food and Agriculture to World Health to UN Women to World Tourism and so on. At the national level, every country has a department or ministry of agriculture that works in agriculture, a department or ministry of education, a department of energy, a department of water and so on – each of which are governed and managed as if they were a world unto themselves.

Institutional Actions Don't Support Systems Solutions

What is worse, the typical organizational climates declare those who dare to try to color outside the boxes in which they are placed as outlaws, heretics, outliers, troublemakers and "unreasonables." (Behold the OHOTU Clan!) This makes organizational change from within fraught with danger. Thus, even when the institution (national or international) has agreed on addressing one of the SDGs, implementation is stymied by the status quo. The organizational rules, regulations, habits, norms and mores, some of which defy common sense, do not support the construct of systems solutions. The inability to support systems solutions is a failure of many dimensions: Structural; Cognitive; Behavioral; Informational; Institutional; and Political. We will discuss the solution in Chapter Six, for now let's look at why we fail.

Individual Cognitive Bias

We can assume that whatever the dimension of the failure, the individual remains the central element owing to the cognitive and behavioral restrictions they are bound by. Let me assure you I have lived this nightmare in my quest to introduce strategic foresight and futures thinking as a planning tool in the august institution where I sojourned in the Department for Sustainable Development. In many countries, there is a lack of data as well as data standardization, but while that is often discussed as the problem, it is not. It is an outcome of the larger problem: the failure of human cognition to take in the whole system. This failure is what makes coherence between government agencies a challenge. We treat each issue or SDG as though it stands alone, when, in reality, this is simply not true.

Deficient Data and Imprudent Decision-Making

This is not to say data or lack thereof is not an issue, it is. Even though there is talk about data-driven policymaking, and decision support, in the realm of public sector, this is not yet the default position. It is not the default position because humans don't use the data, if it exists, and often don't collect the right data because of their rule-bound thinking.

In the case of data for decision-making for the private sector – our Merchant Tribes – the shared rulebook for trade and investment is designed to maximize profit and return on investment for shareholders. These rules most often run contrary to the desire for sustainability. True, we see now rules around carbon disclosure and environmental, social, and governance (ESGs) rules and regulations as sections in annual reports of many of the Fortune 1000 and Standard & Poor's 500 companies, but there is evidence of the strain of grappling with the dissonance that their prime directive or rule is maximize returns on shareholder investment. ESGs are seen as part of corporate social sustainability (CSR) which is a sideline to the main function of the business, window dressing. It does not help that the regulatory bodies for many industries often lack the metrics and measure to monitor and evaluate and the law has only carrot and no bamboo stick for dealing with infractions.

Lack of Foresight
There is also a failure of foresight. Environmental factors like climate change and natural resources management such as water management are often not fully integrated into the long-term business strategy and natural capital and human capital is often not properly valued. How can the Merchant Tribes learn to paint outside the lines of their current borders and boundaries?

Rigid Compartmentalization
When we look at the plural sector – our Caretaker Tribes – it is a painful truth that they have the same tendency to compartmentalize. In the environmental movement, for example, we have ocean people who are in a different boat from

forest people, who are in a different boat from the environmental justice people. And then within the ocean agenda – you find shark people, whale people, coral reef people and turtle people and so on all doing great work in the same ocean but who don't generally talk to each other. How is it that they cannot see they are all waves of the same ocean or sea?

Failures of the Status Quo

Across the board, we can define failure as the gap between what we expect or want, and what actually happens, and there are all sorts of failures that impact on the problem-solving eco-system. For every system challenge addressed by the SDGs, for example, education, health, energy, ocean management, access to finance, there can be design failures, catastrophic failures, compounding failures, human-error failures, and failure to pursue the mandate which can take the form of both actions and inactions on the part of the agency or member state. There is also the failure in leadership, failure of imagination, ethical and moral failure, and failure of foresight. All these failures boil down to two big problems: failure of understanding, and failure of anticipation.

When dealing with complex systems there will always be unavoidable failures, because we cannot fully anticipate how complex systems work, but many failures can be averted by improving design practices. We cannot think in silos and arrive at either sustainability or the sustainable development goals.

Thankfully, the COVIDemic may have precipitated a willingness to rethink what is possible.

A Paradigm Shift Is Needed

As Einstein said, you cannot solve a problem from the same level of consciousness that created it. So, we need to change the level of consciousness.

Problem-solving is part of the problem. For most policy,

program or project design, we use the engineering approach. We define the problem and then solve the problem by finding the immediate cause(s), develop solutions to fix the defined causes, and then implement the solutions. However, once we agree that problems are systems of systems problems, we need to go further. We need to go beyond immediate cause(s) to root sources of the cause(s). And we need to see the dynamic nature of both the problem space and the solution space. This is especially needed for social problems. Problem-solving that looks at root cause analysis or causal layered analysis takes us beneath the tip of the iceberg, which is above the surface that is the litany of the superficial problem definition, to the causes which are systemic such as economic, social or cultural, to the deeper issues that arise from culture and worldviews that inform the system, to the deepest level of metaphors and myths and cosmology that inform the entire system in which the problem is enmeshed.

This type of policy, program and project design helps to improve or clarify our views of both the solution horizon as well as problem situation. We often have data to define the litany, but we often do not have the date or even metrics to define quantitively the things like systems or worldviews or mythologies that underlay the problem. In fact, the worldviews and myths that currently drive what we measure have caused us to fail to collect the data on the real cost of the things we have done and are doing to the environment.

Our economic and investment rulebooks have failed us. This worldview has given rise to the ever-strident opposition to the notion that humans can impact the Earth, and are in fact, impacting the Earth beyond its natural capability to heal itself. This worldview is an outcome of the dominance of market capitalism and WEIRD (that is to say, Western, educated, industrialized, rich and democratic) societies' economics which dominate the psycho-social underpinnings of globalization processes. The Judeo-Christian worldview has been a large contributor to this. By reading from the Bible the construct that "God gave man dominion over the Earth" – we believe that the Earth belongs to mankind as opposed to seeing our species as a part of the Earth – one part of the planetary biome.

"Dominion over" is a root cause at the mythological level of our collective mind – this idea that humans have the ability and right to control God's other creations, both living and non-living. There is a fundamental notion that manna will fall from heaven to save us. Hence the belief (by some) that we cannot run out of water, we cannot run out of space, we cannot run out of fish – because God's world cannot be done. This lack of a belief in the responsibility of humankind for Earth's stewardship has influenced the way we have lived in and exploited the natural world – chopping down trees, mining ores, fracking the Earth for oil – for short-term benefit. It has played out through imperialism and colonialism.

This sense of domination and entitlement is very different from the indigenous peoples' credo that states, "humans belong to the Earth, the Earth does not belong to humans."

We have to envision evolving beyond this paradigm of domination over Mother Nature to a paradigm of restoration and healing with Mother Nature. There are seeds of change happening now. Wales has created a Well-being of Future Generations Act and a Future Generations Commissioner, the first office of its kind in the world, which sets out by law, the processes by which large-scale decisions cannot be made without the study of the long-term impact of future generations. This has caught the imagination of many people around the world. Another seed of change is the Bolivian Law of the Rights of Mother Earth that constitutionally grants plural society or the Caretakers of the environment the right to protest and sue, if necessary, on behalf of Mother Nature – Pacha Mama. The law sent shockwaves around the world. Another seed of change is exemplified by New Zealand courts that after decades of court battle approved a law that gave legal personhood to the Whanganui River, on the basis of Maori traditional culture.

While much of the marketplace has us believing we have lost our sense of community, we see from the development of shared service economy – shared cars, shared tools, shared homes–that people are ready to have and to do something different.

We are ready to reexamine the laws of ecology and how we live with and in Nature. As the Rastafarians say, "Everything is everything." The first Law of Ecology says, "everything is connected to everything else." The second Law of Ecology says that "everything must go somewhere." There is no place called "away." In every natural system, what is excreted by one organism is used by another. There is no waste. We see seeds of change in the push to embrace symbiotic engineering and circular economy and regenerative economy. In symbiotic engineering, industrial zones and industrial parks are designed to operate according to the second law of ecology and the output of one process is the input of another process.

In circular economy there are attempts to measure the lifecycle costs of our consumer goods and services and the true cost of waste, to include, for example, the costs of toxic waste on human health. These ideas are not yet mainstream, but they are there – waiting to be "fed" into our evolving consciousness.

The third Law of Ecology is that "nature knows best." Even though people are paying more attention to nature and using biomimicry as a form of design, they are not getting at the root myth. They are designing insect drones to pollinate fields in case we don't or can't come to our senses in time to save the bees (and other insects that are disappearing such as the dragonfly) and save ourselves. A good seventy percent of the food we eat comes courtesy of the pollination services by bees and other insects, birds and bats. Nature does know best and, so, despite our genius engineering of the Florida everglades, to create spaces for our homes, golf courses, shopping malls and entertainment parks, we see nature rising to reclaim her throne with alligator highway crossings becoming a more common sight and hundred-year floods happening more frequently.

The fourth Law of Ecology states "there is no such thing as a free lunch." We might have thought with all this oil or coal or coltan we're going to be rich, rich, rich, rich. But the fact is, what might be the repercussions of mining on the ecology of the land or the bed of the sea or that asteroid in yonder sky. Said the pet shop owner who released the lionfish into the Caribbean Sea, "it's just a couple of little-little fish, what harm could that do in the big-big Sea?" Now that the parrot fish that clean the reefs are near extinction, we know the dangers of each person believing erroneously that they have no responsibility for the greater good. A failure of morals.

We have killed off enough species, felled enough trees, decimated enough fish and extracted minerals at a rate that goes beyond the capacity of Pacha Mama to replenish. There's a kind of callousness, a lack of humility for our unknown unknowns that really has to be canceled, as we say in the vernacular. Some in the Merchant Tribes are asking the question, "How can business be a force for good?" They are asking can we create value for the communities in which we do business? Can we treat the water we use to process the chemicals we make as revered and ensure we return that water the same or better than when we got it? Some are interrogating the race for Space. They want to be sure that this does not devolve to a quest for bragging rights among buccaneer-boy billionaires, but rather that our extra-terrestrial cogitations and plans value Space as a sustainable resource for all humanity. The questions are being asked, will we explore the Space frontier with the same winner-takes-all-no-matter-what mentality of the past 500 years? What lessons have we learnt that might take us humbly into this most exciting venture? Can we learn to say, "we belong to the cosmos, the cosmos does not belong to us?"

If only we can move the status quo from its inertia, to move from shareholder primacy, as a driver for capitalism, to all stakeholder primacy, we will change our paradigm. For years, indigenous people have been pleading and throwing themselves on the mercy of the powers that be to no avail. We need a shift in some of the rules of the global governance architecture handed down over the last five hundred years. If we learn nothing from the COVID-19 pandemic we should learn that the future of many things, like viruses, may not recognize what we consider a border or boundary. Not to be pessimistic but given the mystery of the "bird flu," I will confess that I have spent some time in the rabbit hole of mutating viruses spread by migrating birds.

We need a paradigm shift. One that involves 10 percent of the "WE" who want a sustainable future. We in the public sector, private sector, and plural civil sector. This paradigm shift will help us address our failures by improving our problem-solving ecosystem. It will help us ask better questions of our future such as how we share the planet, how we share our humanity, how we share our rulebook, and how we share our decision-making.

Making a Paradigm Shift

This idea of making a paradigm shift is a serious matter because it is not a simple thing to make that shift. A paradigm shift is a change. Change is challenging for human beings. All change. Radical Change. Developmental Change. Remedial Change. Incremental Change. Transformational Change. Changing our paradigms will impact our systems and vice-versa. We need to address structural change, process and procedures change, people and culture change.

We are talking about a change in the way we understand how we share the planet. The Earth does not belong to human beings. Human beings belong to the Earth. We are talking about a change in how we share our humanity – our education, health care, and other social systems. We are talking about a change in our rulebooks. The rules by which the global economy operates. The shift from Newtonian understanding of physics, to quantum theory was a major shift. Likewise, our economic theories have to make a paradigm shift from a Newtonian view of the world to a quantum view of the world. We are still using economic theorems that existed before stock trading could be done in microseconds and a book was delivered as a file on a screen on my smartphone. This fact seems to have escaped the notice of the many economists who remain wedded to the covenant of the GDP while touting the vision of sustainable development. These do not compute.

We need a change in how we share decision-making. Who is at the table, who decides the agenda, who decides the language of the agenda? Decisions made today will impact the future of GenZers now in high school who are now living with COVID. No wonder they are the ones marching to the beat of their frustration and outrage at our seeming ineptitude. They are ready to make the paradigm shift. We know this because we can see how the trend to a sharing economy is rising, as is concern with work-life balance. They understand that wellbeing matters and the value of a Gross National Happiness Index. Why have the burden of a car with insurance, parking costs, and the like when you can jump, walk, ride your bike, jump on a train or hail a cab or rideshare service? The COVIDemic has heightened our sense of life's fragility and made more people of all ages awaken to the truth that shopping is not the key to a fulfilled life. Despite the naysayers who state that the COVIDemic has set back achieving the SDGs by 30 years, or more, I believe the opposite. I am among the body of the hopeful that believe that the seeds of transformation that have been planted over the last five years if tended can multiply in abundance. The call for transformational engineering, transformational thinking and transformational leadership has been sounded and are being echoed in ways that can amplify and resonate to catch fire.

According to the Rensselaer Polytechnic Institute study which informs my theory of change, we need ten percent of a society believing in something before an emerging idea becomes the new norm. The researchers studied movements such as the women's movement, the environmental movement, and the same sex marriage movement to arrive at this conclusion. So, what needs to happen now is that there needs to be (and this is my number) 11% of the people who have a global consciousness to make the transformational shift. How many is that? Depends on how you count, of course. But let us say 500 million which would be near 11 percent of the 4.9 billion of us who have a smartphone, and almost 25 percent of the Facebook users around the world as of 2019.

As the agents of our destiny on this Planet Earth, we must become smarter if we are to live in the futures we want – futures of flourishing. Smart cities. Smart cars. Smart houses. How about Smart futures? But what does that mean? And how can we translate that in a way that is helpful to us to become better agents of change and make the change for the better world that we want? A world that is sustainable—within the planetary boundaries. How do we get from the hornets' nest of challenges to a beehive of solutions? What if we could get 11% of the world to think and use the words "Smart Futures"? Who remembers who first used the words smart phone? It doesn't matter because whoever coined the word "smartphone" had a sticky word that took hold. A paradigm shift happens when a sticky idea – a meme – is spread. The "Smart" meme already exists. We all know that there are many different possible and plausible and preferred futures. Why not embrace "Smart futures" as a way to improve our decision-making?

It is a well-known truism that having a shared vision is critical to successful changemaking. People need images of the desired future. These images should appeal to the varied stakeholders.

Without that shared vision, it is not easy to get change to take hold and to turn each person into a connector and/or changemaker. The vision must, of necessity, be a coherent, and compelling narrative of where you are heading. In other words, we need myths and stories to change our paradigms. The application of a SMART Futures thinking, or framework could help with the visioning, and would be the new paradigm. It would allow us to rehearse the futures so that we can better design ways to get there. It would address barriers to change like strategic shortcomings, underestimating scale and scope, neglected stakeholders, lack of trust, pessimism because of past failed change efforts, lack of tooling, lack of endurance and inertia. This paradigm shift is called the Smart Futures Framework for sustainable design, and it addresses the problem-solving ecosystem from the design of policies to programs, to projects. This framework enables anyone, anywhere — working on any issue — to address complex challenges through the same lens and provide a common framing for moving the process from hornets' nest of problems to beehive of solutions. Just think, with five questions, we can all "Get SMART."

Day Four
The Year 2050
Anansi Attends Indigenous Peoples Convocation with Grandmother Spider

August 9, 2050, UN Day of Indigenous Peoples
Maya Long Count Date l 13.1.18.3.5

Celebratory Remarks
Faja-Dan Aboikoni, Queen Mother, Saramacca People

Today is the UN Day of Indigenous Peoples and I am one of only three "haole" invited to speak at the Launch of the 2070 Covenant of the Indigenous Peoples. I am preparing for the presentation I will make at the Dreamtime Conclave. It is rare for someone who is not indigenous to be invited to speak, much less at the Dreamtime Conclave which is their cosmic matters assembly.

The 2070 Covenant will build on the successes and failures of the 2050 Agreement we launched back in 2030. By 2030, as a result of our global women's movement revived after COVID, there were thirty-five countries with women as heads of state. This was due to both the evidence of competent handling of the COVID-19 pandemic by women Leaders and the rising economic clout of women in the marketplace. The COVID-19 pandemic era helped to birth a new kind of social/sustainable capitalism – focused on people, planet, purpose, and prosperity, when many corporations began to build stakeholder concerns into their determination of shareholder value. This was providential as a second wave of pandemic hit (thankfully better anticipated and managed) in 2025. By then some of the children of the Future Friday climate change movement had gained the right to vote and the new day was dawning. Back in 2030 I had been honored as an Indigenous People's Ancestor when I became a spokesperson for Space Sustainability and the Movement for the passing of a Global Space Covenant to update the UN Outer Space Treaty to reflect the new reality of twenty-first-century Space exploration.

Despite all efforts, we are a world under pressure as the numbers of climate migrants and refugees rise. Among the ten largest countries worldwide, Nigeria has become the third largest country in the world, behind China and India. The Ubuntu Agenda has gone global, and we have successfully managed to create a community economic system that has reduced unrest in both Asia and Africa. Indeed, there has been a marked decrease in violent gun crimes since the year 2030 and considering 2030 was a time of war upon war, the last twenty years have been a relatively peaceful period for humanity. The peace dividend has resulted in massive investments in education and health, and water and sanitation, and so the investments in integrated rural and urban community development have been much more impactful and this is in large part because of the shift to the Wellbeing Index. Indeed, the Wellbeing Index of Botswana, Ghana, Malawi, and all the small island developing states are far above even that of the USA even though their global GDP rankings remain low. Most of Africa, the Caribbean and Pacific have converted to Wellbeing metrics over the last 25 years following the global launch in 2025. Several cities are now carbon neutral like Austin, Accra, Barcelona, Berlin, Boston, Buenos Aires, Cape Town, Caracas, Copenhagen, Durban, London, Los Angeles, Melbourne, Mexico City, Milan, New York City, Oslo, Paris, Philadelphia, Portland, Quito, Rio de Janeiro, Salvador, San Francisco, Santiago, Seattle, Stockholm, Sydney, Toronto, Vancouver, Washington, and Yokohama.

Forty years ago, my honorary godfather , a Mayan Priest, addressed this gathering. He stated that All of humanity must work together to re-establish harmony and unity with the natural environment by implementing the Kyoto Protocol and creating a global governance system that respected and supported vegetable, mineral, animal, human and cosmic life. At the time, global Leaders planned to review the Kyoto Protocol in 2012, the same year as the thirteenth B'Aqtun or 5,200 years of the Maya people, a year which, according to Maya wisdom, would usher in a new era of respect for others, love, solidarity, and kinship, a change for humanity to think about the future of the human race and Mother Earth. To understand that Mother Earth, Pacha Mama, was alive. To understand that she was the mother of all beings that coexisted on the planet and that all the universe is alive and interconnected. That "Earth does not belong to human beings. Human beings belong to the Earth." That "the Cosmos do not belong to human beings. Human beings belong to the Cosmos." But that transition would require a spiritual strength that humanity did not have until after the second pandemic hit in 2025.

It was not until 2025 that this wisdom took deep roots and spread the notion that scientific research should recognize the spiritual dimensions of human beings, the connection and interconnectedness of all the elements of the universe, and that much of the imbalance, climate change, global warming, environmental crisis, and threat to biological and cultural diversity were the result of the endemic financial, monetary, and commercial system. It took time for the status quo to agree that the history and experience of the "economic pluralism" and productive models of indigenous peoples' cultures provided a new departure for fleeing the old ways and pursuing sanctuary in new ways of being in the world. We used to say then we are moving "AWKward" into the future. AWK-ward meaning advancing within knowing-ward with humility recognizing the truth of the many unknown unknowns in the human fields of knowing.

My honorary godfather as far back as 2020, faced down conventional wisdom that stated that we could not achieve global sustainability, by denouncing the lure of self-fulfilling prophecy and calling on all spiritual warriors throughout the world to weave together a new story. Thus, the SMART Futures and the Regenerative Economy and the Just Space and other movements came together to form what we lovingly call the OHOTU Clan. We – Outliers, Heretics, Outlaws, Troublemakers and "Unreasonables" – came together fleeing madness and the thrall of technological self-extinction to revitalize wisdom and knowledge through new alliances, coalitions and strategies to promote the sustainable development at all levels of life, which respect animal, mineral, human and cosmic life and ensure the future of mankind.

What will our world look like in 20 years? In 2070 when we celebrate the one hundredth Anniversary of Earth Day and the fortieth anniversary of the Space Justice proclamation launched on December 10th Human Rights Day in 2030. At 89 years old, I will not be alive to see it.

Many fear the worst. Today as violent storms rip through the world, we are barely holding on to the crop biodiversity we have gained by spreading the urban homesteading movement. Despite efforts, large numbers of people continue suffering from chronic food insecurity, not because of lack of food. Indeed, the food waste movements over the last thirty years since the Great Pause have made significant inroads into the issue of ending food waste. The issue was one of lack of resources to secure even distribution. The number of climate refugees seems to be growing faster than our ability to manage it. Some people are calling for reopening talks on solar geoengineering to address climate change, but thanks to our Space Futures Games we have been able to help people tour that future and what they see has prompted the meme, "Don't mess with Father Sun. Your arms are too short to box with the Gods," you see on T-shirts everywhere.

Our biggest hope is that we continue to promote SMART futures literacy across the board. Today we will announce the opening of the "My World 2070" tour on the Futures Holodeck which is the fourth update since we began the My World Future Tours exhibit that had first been mounted in 2025 on the fringes of the World Bank Annual meetings. Our Holodeck uses virtual reality to simulate a view of what our lives might be like if we do nothing to address the number of challenges we face. We have built out images of a home, an office, a store, a place of worship, a court, and so on so people can experience how they will live – eat, sleep, work, waste, heal, love, play, pray in this future.

Our first Futures Holodeck was designed by the Ubuntu Alliance in partnership with a Consortium of Universities that had Futures Labs. It was created to assist designers to better imagine what we *might need to live in a future world where elements of climate change have created changes in the arc of cities and lives and where robots and AI enhancements have already occurred. The Futures Holodeck is viewed as part of the Space Futures Games designed to help in promoting futures literacy and support the project on How We Share the Future 2030 plus. Based on the philosophy embodied in the SMART Futures Framework, the holo-deck takes what's happening now and fast-forwards the action to the future you want to explore. Many of the inventions you see today were first experienced on the holodeck, like the SMART health app built into a bra, we invented to detect the beginnings of a heart attack in women and advise them to seek treatment immediately. This technology helped us to secure the 2030 Just Space Futures Covenant which treats critical issues related to how we share Space, like the rules for asteroid or extra-planetary mining for the elements – that are fundamental to modern civilization: gold, silver, platinum, iridium, cadmium, osmium in a way that benefits all humanity. Today, people rely on our FPS (Futures Positioning System) to review and rehearse the consequences of their decisions. That is the hope I have for our future. And that is the gospel message I come to bring.*

Chapter 4

How Might We Cultivate a Paradigm Shift?

James Allen in the book *As a Man Thinketh* notes, "A man cannot directly choose his circumstances, but he can choose his thoughts, and so indirectly, yet surely, shape his circumstances." And, paraphrasing in deference to the politically correct norms of our day that "all that one achieves and all that one fails to achieve is the direct result of one's thoughts." We are enmeshed in a system where all the rules, all the processes, are geared towards the primacy of financial profit. What we are really addressing are wicked social problems, which means problems with the agents impacting and being impacted in different ways by other problems and agents. This means even when people are actually operating to achieve the same goal, they can't find common ground to diagnose the problems because the problems are so interdependent, they are inseparable.

The implicit bias of human training often leaves people blind to some spots. Each one seeing only one part of the elephant. As such, problems are ill-diagnosed, misdiagnosed and/ or undiagnosed. Changing the problem-solving approach is not a simple thing since our approach itself is deeply rooted in our worldview – born out of the eco-philosophy that "Man must dominate the Earth." Stewardship is seen to be in service of monetary wealth creation and retention. To arrive at sustainability as a planetary civilization, what we need is both a revolutionary and evolutionary paradigm shift. Having and changing the goals is critically important also, however, changing the mindset, or paradigm, out of which the whole system – that is, goals, structures, rules, parameters – arises, as well as having the power to transcend the dominant paradigms, is necessary first and foremost.

At one time, for example, the world was believed to be flat, then came a paradigm shift that says, "No, the world is round." People died for believing in, and advocating for, that shift. Then there was the paradigm that said the Sun revolves around the Earth, then came a shift that took us to saying, "the Earth revolves around the sun." Some people were excommunicated for that shift. More recently, we experienced a paradigm shift when we moved from a world defined by Newtonian physics to one described by quantum physics. Likewise, at the social level, in our recent time, we have seen a paradigm shift which ushered in the era of same-sex marriage – now legal in several countries. We know we are capable of making these shifts, and now we need to do it with shared sense of urgency of purpose.

Short-Termism

As we think about the ideas and behaviors we practice and value, one of the first shifts we have to make is the move away from short-termism as a way of thinking, being and planning. Our obsession with short-termism means that our societies create mistakes that drive instability and unsustainability as we measure and value short-term results over long-term gains. "Eat, drink and be merry today because tomorrow is promised to no one" is our preferred refrain. This earworm has burrowed into our subconscious, so that in healthcare we reward fixes and clean-ups rather than upfront investments in prevention; hence insurance policies that don't reimburse for preventative care. The culture is one of "Let's pay to fix it," as opposed to, "Let's pay to prevent it." Short-termism is a failure of imagination that dances happily with policy and planning which is focused on two-year, and four-year election and profit cycles.

Revolution and Evolution

A paradigm shift is not a cake walk. It is hard for transformational change to happen. We are largely creatures of habit. "We have always done it this way" is our go-to position. Hence, we need a combination of revolution and evolution to move the status quo. We need the revolution from above and below, as well as evolution from within and without. Transformational change requires both.

"Revolution" usually means to "overthrow" and while we may not want to overthrow totally what was, we do need to throw out the old metrics and other rulebooks that no longer serve us. "Evolution" means a process of change – growth – that is formed over time, that usually comes from within. We as human beings evolve from a sperm and an egg. Our bodies are in a constant state of regeneration. We are not the same body we were seven years ago even if our DNA remains the same.

In order to happen, paradigm shifts demand a combination of both revolutionary and evolutionary change. We have rulebooks and wish lists calling for all kinds of revolutionary changes such as our carbon emission targets and plastic bans but until we have an accompanying evolutionary change in mindset, where a sustainability mindset actually becomes the norm, we will continue to tinker at the edges of the problems. We want companies to think about the design of new products, the design of new factories and industries. We want them to think about industrial symbiosis. We want politicians to see themselves as good stewards of nature and make the better choice for sustainability long-term every time. Not just for the sake of virtue signaling, but because fundamentally they get the reality that we literally are all in this together.

Organizations must become very good at structuring the change process to achieve transformation, and because we're talking about multiples of organizations and institutions, there's no one-size-fits-all. "System of systems" thinking is the bedrock of this evolutionary change and likewise, unfortunately, we also have the habit of avoiding thinking about things we do not feel good about. As we ramp up in this Industry 4.0 World, driven by the innovations in information, nano and neuro technology and the like, we will be faced with even more bewildering and even dangerous decisions.

So, when we think about organizational paradigm shifts, we need to think about the structure which is the architecture of the organization, the routines and processes of the organization, the tangible and intangible resources of the organization, as well as the organizational knowledge and value, and finally, the behavior of the individuals in that organization. What are the beliefs about this organization, the industry in which it is embedded? All these elements are required to make a paradigm shift. Everything is interconnected; we can't get out of it, around it or under it. There are five kinds of thinking styles needed to cultivate a paradigm shift and these are not in any form of hierarchy. While I have broken these thinking styles down for purposes of explanation, please understand that they are mutually reinforcing behaviors for sustainable design – like the flour, sugar, eggs, fat, leavening agent any baker needs for a cake. We need them all together.

Futures Thinking

First, futures thinking. We need to create a flourishing future through a culture of sustainable choice-making. We need to get literate regarding thinking about the future 10, 20, and 30 years from now. We need to be comfortable with the idea that we live in a volatile, uncertain, complex and ambiguous world that may turn out to be very different from where we are now because of all the changes emerging in the landscape around us. We have to be able to hold a gaze that goes beyond the election cycle, or your next annual bonus, recognize that as the life cycle of most capital infrastructure investment in homes, commercial real estate, roads and bridges are 30 years, at the very least, we should be able to mentally travel back and forth on a thirty-year time horizon. Futures thinking takes us to "what if" questions that engage our mind in creating scenarios that help us to address many of the unquantifiable issues in the meshwork of the systems we are trying to problem-solve for. Futures thinking allows us to make leaps of imagination and non-linear connections between the agents in the system and perform story making, or narratives, which help us to better rehearse the many variations of possible futures. In the real world, we observe seeds of change such as the Wellbeing of Future Generations Act in Wales, complete with the Future Generations Commissioner, who oversees policy decisions that impact on their goals for a more prosperous Wales, a resilient Wales, a more equal Wales, a healthier Wales, a Wales of cohesive communities, and a Wales of vibrant culture and thriving Welsh language. This system is now being studied by many other communities and cities and nations around the world to see how this might work for them. In the wake of COVID-19, we have an increase in the demand to promote futures thinking widely in order to address what are seen as logjams in the move to sustainability. The goal is to bring "futures literacy" to a wide body of people around the world and to ensure this capability for Leaders and planners everywhere so that we can look beyond the -ism of the hour and move towards the futures we want. We need that capability for futures thinking to inform all decision-making such as clean water for all and waste management and recycling. We need futures thinking that promotes the circular and regenerative economy so that we can see more clearly the options of the futures emerging in the landscape around us. Futures thinking is certainly one thinking style that is critical to flourishing.

Interdependent Thinking

Second, is interdependent thinking. Science has shown that there's such a thing as a social brain. Human evolution, – because we don't have any fur, we don't have natural claws, big teeth like dogs and wolves, etc. — has required we cooperate and form clans, Tribes, communities and nations in order to survive. Interdependence is not a foreign idea. The problem is that the market world we live in has focused on and promoted individualism as the way to success. "Somebody has to win, and somebody has to lose" is the mantra of the individualistic, WEIRD societies that have dominated the formation of the "global rules book" writing. A seed of change is emerging in the sharing economy and in the technology community because people necessarily build off each other. They recognize a value in seeking collegiality and drawing on each other's resources. Even though there is still competition, it is a collaborative competition. Conflict is seen as valuable in this form of interdependence; differences are managed in a productive way. This is more prevalent in more collaborative cultures, where conflict is first to be avoided through dialogue. We have to understand the power of dialogue and create more space in organizations, and governance structures that allow us to practice how to collaborate inter and intra sector and industry. Even intra organization, Leaders will need to intentionally demonstrate interdependence, which will demand policy change as some companies are set up to compete even inside the company. That is to say, the organization is not designed to foster cross-collaboration between silos, they are set up to compete for resources. What is needed is a kind of leadership mindset that allows the practice of collaboration by the Leaders themselves, such that they are able to take risks, share budgets differently, ask questions that they themselves don't know the answer to in public. We need Leaders who can see a world without borders or boundaries, to breakdown or stand up to the borders and boundaries we have created across profession, city, country, and "-ism" of choice.

Even in groups that purport to work on the same "issue-ism" there are boundaries. For example, within the "ocean protection-ism," there are coral reef people separate from whale people, separate from turtle people working on the same ocean who never come into contact even when policy issues pertaining to the management of the whole are being addressed. We have a whole set of boundaries that have to be unlearned or bridged. You have to be able to tap into the power of differentiation and see the value in that, to get to win-win, a popular term now, which can benefit from rethinking, as indeed, a coin has three sides not two. This kind of shapeshifting requires a new story for shaping the future we want.

Transgenerational Thinking

Third, is transgenerational thinking. We are experiencing an intergenerational workplace which ranges from Boomers to Generation X to Millennials, Generation Y, Next, Z, and Generation Alpha who will be alive and well in 2100. Beyond the 2100 expiry date, the thinking of the futures of those who are not in the room yet – the futures yet unborn, the century 2500 or 3000 might be accomplished by thinking about your own life and asking what kind of ancestor you want to be. The term ancestor here applies not just to our blood relatives, but all human beings as a class of species. We might take note of the fact that the children who have been marching for climate change, see a disaster on the horizon based on our current trajectory – without natural bees or trees. Their call for future justice is now being amplified by the COVIDemic which has laid bare the potential disaster looming in the face of accelerating biodiversity loss which will create increased pressure on the millions of viruses safely ensconced in the virus-sphere to leave their current abode and move into ours.

There are bright spots and seeds of change like the laws in New Zealand, Bolivia and Ecuador which have brought into our consciousness the possibility of creating laws to protect Nature, as well as the climate lawsuit *Juliana, et al. v. **United States of America, et al.*** filed in 2015 by 21 youth plaintiffs against the United States and several executive-branch officials in order to act as a "guardian for future generations." Given the improvements in health care, there is a significant possibility that they will be sprightly way beyond the year 2100, giving fuel to the idea that we have only just begun to see the sprouting of legal approaches. Transgenerational thinking puts into practice the Seventh Generation Principle from the founding document of the Iroquois Confederacy, the oldest living participatory democracy on Earth that states: "In our every deliberation, we must consider the impact of our decisions on the next seven generations."

Teleos Thinking

This takes us to the idea of teleological thinking. The first time I heard the word "teleological" was in my Industrial Engineering Technology assessment class and I fell madly in love. The word featured prominently in my dissertation which addressed the less than effective outcome of many of the large-scale projects funded by the development finance industry. Countless stories have been told of white elephants and mothballed projects that represent unholy debt for developing countries, stories of well-meaning transfers of "stuff" and development projects from the global North to the global South that fail to launch. *Teleos* thinking (the word *teleo* is a Greek word which means the "ultimate aim" or the "ultimate purpose") is about ensuring that we're asking the question to what end? The focus of teleos thinking and teleological design becomes how to achieve the stated ends, how to reduce the distance between the current state and the established purpose. The gap between what was intended and what is achieved, I define as the development effectiveness gap. Teleological design is aimed at narrowing the gap between the emerging problem space and the emerging solution space.

When we're doing a policy, program or project investment,

there's a problem space that we're trying to affect. It could be healthcare, education, transportation, water system, energy, whatever – traditional project design and evaluation methodologies call for hindsight data, that is historic data which is projected into the future. Typically, there is insufficient attention to anticipatory design, and no reference to either the evolution of the solution space or the problem itself. Thus, by the time you've built the project solution, the problem space already has changed, thus creating a development effectiveness gap. Teleological design would allow us to do a better job of filling that gap. Teleological thinking supports design in very powerful ways through asking "What is the problem we're trying to solve?" "What might the problem be like in the future?" "What does the solution look like?" This helps us describe the distance between what is and what it is we want.

Narrative Thinking

Effective changemaking demands an ability to communicate a vision, hope, desire for a future that does not yet exist. We need the critical skills of being able to imagine, define and describe the desired outcome of the process or project or policy. Story has the power to engage the listener. Scientific research has shown that a story lights up many more parts of the brain and creates neural pathways that allow for greater retention by the listener. In the case of complex problem-solving, a story allows us to address the mindset or root cause of "wicked" problems in ways that are not possible using mathematical equations. Story is a very powerful way of collapsing "system of systems" problems into very easily graspable ideas that people can process, analyze, and then design responses to. Hence, in this book I use story to envision the future and look back at us from various vantage points to which we would not have access in any other way.

A paradigm shift for a flourishing future demands change at

the level of the individual, the social, and at the organizational, which in turn requires an ability to communicate a shared vision. It is not likely we will be able to move mass change needed to accomplish any of the goals of the SDGs by talking about change in percentages or indices. We will need to find ways to share the vision for the change we want to see. In 2050, the headline story would read, for example, "This pilot kindergarten school feeding program that began back in 2030 has reaped dividends, as the number of elementary children at grade 3 level who are able to perform above average on their critical thinking skills test has increased threefold over 2030. Now, the challenge is to increase the access of nutritional food to reach 100 percent of all kindergarten children in Africa by 2070."

In fact, I think stories like this can be told about any subject whatsoever to do with the sustainable development goals. There is power in storytelling. The body of literature substantiates the power of story to stimulate emotional response. Stories are very efficient at transmitting complex ideas, and to encourage a mindset shift. It is a different kind of leverage to use storytelling in the public sector, in the private sector, in the plural civil society, to talk about the sustainable futures we want to see, as things that have occurred. We are able to hold the tensions between the different competing ideas, different competing voices, different competing interests in a story, and actually work through it much easier than if we were to use the logical side of the brain.

Story allows us to rehearse the future we want. According to neurobiologists Dr. William Calvin and Dr. David Ingvar, our drive to tell stories about our future is hardwired into our human brain and is closely linked to our ability to speak and construct language. Rehearsing the future creates a "future memory." This brain power of imagination can be used to "rehearse" optimal performance outcomes, your goals, dreams, and future. Your thoughts are a powerful energy linked to your beliefs. They produce imagery in your mind that shape and direct the chemical reactions in every cell in your body. When a positive emotional energy state displaces a negative one, it has the power to permanently transform limiting beliefs. This process directs your subconscious mind, the part of the brain that controls the autonomic functions of the body, to create new neural pathways that will be open to support you in the future that you want to create.

Thus, in my own work, to conjure a paradigm shift on the issue of anti-black racism in Latin America and in the development assistance community, I made a conscious decision to adopt a storytelling and a futures approach, to enable me to hold what were very challenging conversations as the only black person and the most junior person in the room and speaking truth to power. Stories allowed for the creation of a mutually safe landing place where we could reach out in honesty to describe the problem space of inequality and the situation at hand and helped me advance the cause of the "Black" agenda and make allies among my white colleagues who had previously tried hard to avoid both me and the issue.

SMART Futures

We are at a point of transition. We might choose to see this Great Pause of the COVIDemic as an unwanted gift horse, because of the tectonic shifts it has brought into play, such as working from home. The consensus used to be that everyone could not work from home. Now that we have gotten used to not sitting in traffic jams, most people do not want to return to work the way they used to. They want some blend of both. This crisis is an optimal opportunity for a global conversation on the future we want and how we might shape it together. People are looking for a new way forward. Many have lost or are losing faith in traditional leadership and are now looking to their peers for inspiration. There is an unspoken agreement about our shared consciousness of the need to reset our future. It is important that we ask, what is our footprint? But we must also ask, what is our handprint? How will we make the course correction each time to right thoughts, right feelings, right words, right actions, and right reactions until this way of being in the world becomes the norm?

How do we get people to make a shift, to adopt this new mindset? What way will make these ideas around problem-solving stick? How do we get the numbers to a tipping point? According to Dan Heath, author of the book *Made to Stick*, there are six principles that make ideas sticky. They must be simple, concrete, credible, unexpected, emotional, and make a good story. The premise of the SMART Futures is to provide a sticky framework. Just think, over 4.9 billion people carry a smartphone. And all around the world, we are planning for Smart cities, Smart cars, Smart Houses, Smart Energy, Smart HealthCare. What if we could plan for SMART Futures? What if we all agreed on what SMART really meant? What if we could define SMART through five effective questions that could help people to change how they tackle problem-solving? Five questions that are simple, concrete, credible, unexpected, emotional, and that help us to make a good story? Five smart questions that when asked to create an acronym for the word SMART as a mnemonic for the principles:

S = sustainable systems
M= moral metrics
A=anticipatory agency
R= robust resilience
T=transformational technology.

Five questions that could make the way to a teleologically effective problem-solving framework accessible to anyone designing projects, programs, policies, processes, or products.

Could five questions help us learn to unlearn what no longer serves us and provide a path to reframing our view of the world in ways that get us closer to improved teleological effectiveness in the choices we make? Einstein said that we cannot solve our problems with the same thinking we used when we created them. Clearly our time calls for a paradigm shift. What if we could shape this through seeking for SMART Futures?

Day Five
The Year 2040
Anansi Visits the Communications Chair for Smart Planet Collaboratory on World Water Day

March 22, Freetown, Sierra Leone

Text of Transcript of Online Conversation between Asenata Gyurly, Communications Chair, SMART Planet Collaboratory and another Board Member Darby Alma (who are both fitted with augmentation hardware for hearing and sight).

Asenata: Do we have anyone in Dubai, who can cover the World Water Congress Opening Session today? Because we need live footage of the Ubuntu Alliance Street Action as B-roll. Are you in contact with them over there? My bandwidth is really slow right now because I have the holodeck I work in open.

Darby: Yes. We have two freelancers who do both drone and VR footage who could do it for our budget. The connection is spotty though. Not sure why. Usually feed from Dubai is clean. What I might want to do is to use their mass reenactment as a backdrop for the arc of the second segment of our story. I think the visual of a 100,000 people dressed in costumes each printed with 100,000 eyes to represent the 1 billion people in the world is really a powerful metaphor for showing these Leaders that the eyes of the world are on them if they don't sign on to the 2050 Treaty to address the Right to Water.

Asenata: I don't think they will. That's why we need that footage to complete this series of videos. We need to get some tension into the story justifying the solutions we have identified in the SMART Water Innovation Labs.

Darby: So, the sequence is the youth groups in the Refugee Camps building the water recycling facilities, then the megacity engineers waste-water treatment plants; and then the micro desalination plants used on small island developing states interspersed with clips from the speech *Alpha Luna* in 2030. Let me run the clip I picked.

TRANSCRIPT FROM FILM Clip of 2030 World Water Day: We anticipate that despite our efforts water will become a major stressor by 2040. Thirty of the most water-stressed nations will be in Africa and the Middle East. Some will be extremely highly stressed with a score of 5.0 out of 5.0, like Bahrain, Palestine, Israel, and Lebanon. We believe that water balance is possible, and, yes, we know that the regional violence and political turmoil commanding global attention makes our preoccupation with water seem tangential. It is not. Thirty years after the Syrian civil war began, people are still living on the margins and that is about water. Even the United States, China and India face water risks of their own. But our SMART Water Labs have shown us ways in which to make what we have do more for us. Our vision for water remains clear.

Asenata: The vision piece is vital, but we really must use the quote. About the Global Water Guardians. That has the bite we need.

Darby: It's a bit Long… "In the past ten years, since the Holy Transition called for by the COVID-19 pandemic, we the citizens of the global community have never been more awake and sensitive to our individual and collective duty to humanity, Mother Nature and the Earth in general. Our eyes are on you Leaders. All over the world, we are clamoring for a better reality: For our endangered species, for our children, for our climate, for our future. We will wage peace everywhere until our vision is fulfilled. Today, on World Water Day, 2030, we launch the Global Water Guardians Movement. We are a chorus of harmonized voices who say to you… Our eyes are on you. We won't watch and wait. We will watch and work. We call on Leaders to follow us. We know where we are going even if you don't. Our eyes are on you. Ad Futura."

Asenata: Right! That is a bit long. Can we break it up? Or, Oh Dear! This just came into my newsfeed. A Space mission was all set out to retrieve the XU-10 cubesat which was sending an unusual signal back to Lunarville. Scientists were very excited because it looked like a proof of unusually strong life activities in an unknown planet in Sombrero galaxy. But right after sending the signal, the connection to the Moon station was lost. So, it was being retrieved manually to collect data. But nothing has gone according to the plan. An unpredicted solar storm hit. Many satellites have been lost. Space Stations on Earth lost connection with the Lunarville.

Darby: I switched to Global News Network... a village in the hinterlands of Honduras has been hit. A big chunk of Space debris has hit the village. They are not sure of the number, but casualties could be in the hundreds because it was a festival day for the community.

Asenata: They have lost contact with the research station on Lunarville. Wow. They don't know the status. I just hope they are okay up there. Lunarville took us forever as a civil society to get funding.

Darby: Listen to this. "They anticipate it will be at least 48 hours before the connection between Lunarville and us on Earth can be restored." Uh Oh. There is a power failure to the surrounding communities affected by the satellite's crash. I better go charge my batteries. In case we lose power here in Costa Rica. We have a regional grid. Without power, I cannot see.

Asenata: I have been telling you to get a micro solar pack generator since they came out two years ago. What are you waiting for? Anyway. Let's shutdown this session on the Virtua-Meet. Add this last sentence at the end of the clip using the voice synthesizer so we have it in a multiple voice frame: "Problems do not go away by sweeping them under the rug. This is why we, the World Water Guardians, are calling on the powers of the world to join with us to adequately protect our water supply and safeguard out futures for our coming generations on this planet, our home. We demand research funds equal to that spent on the search for water on Mars. We demand the Water Treaty 2050 be adopted and funded. Our eyes are on you." We can use the footage from the Conference as B-Roll there. Let's wrap up so we can prepare for the aftermath of the solar flare. Ad Futura.

Darby: Ubuntu.

Chapter 5

What Is the Smart Futures Framework?

How do we move from now to next?

Now that we know that our thinking has to shift to create a flourishing future we envision, what can we do to shift our thinking?

Despite the fact we know change is constant – all the cells in our bodies change every seven years more or less – we tend to resist change. Neuroscience says we can do SMART things to help people make change possible. We know learning is enhanced by using humor, storytelling, movement, and games which stimulate the brain's emotional center, the amygdala, so that we can process new material more efficiently and effectively. Effective problem-solvers are both born and made. Effective problem-solvers learn to adopt a mindset that sees the most seemingly intractable problems as tangled skeins of a beautiful tapestry yet to be made. Effective problem-solvers see order in the most convoluted hornets' nest. Effective problem-solvers use all the neuroscience to bring change and they do it in a SMART way.

The SMART Futures framework is a process that can help shape that mindset. Implicit in the framework are mutually reinforcing approaches to "complex systems solutioneering" underlying the success application of this framework:

1. being ever-curious about every element of a problem;
2. being imperfectionists, with a high tolerance for ambiguity;
3. having a "dragonfly eye" view of the world, to see through multiple lenses;
4. tapping into the collective intelligence of all in the

ecosystem and bringing them into the room;

5. practicing "show and tell," because storytelling helps drive change.

We need to move beyond the outdated echo chamber that characterizes Western leadership thinking through unlocking evolutionary or smart intelligence. Meaning, we need to get to leadership that is driven by an activated combination of spiritual, moral, analytical, relational and telos or temporal intelligence. This is critical because it is well known that "He who knows not and knows not that he knows not is a fool. Shun him."

A paradigm shift demands something of both the members of the high court, and the great unwashed. It demands we breakdown borders and boundaries between the edges of the different movements – environmental justice and climate and anti-racism and gender and water and food security and so on. People have been talking about the need for a paradigm shift for a long time. There are hectares of forests in print in testimony to that. The ideas of Sustainable Systems, Meaningful Metrics, Anticipatory Agency, Robust Resilience, and Transformational Technology – have been around in one form or another. But when taken together, these words form an acronym, SMART, and the basic construct for the global future of flourishing we want to co-create.

The SMART Futures Framework proposes viewing a complex problem space through the lens of five principles addressed as questions. Everywhere. Every time. Everyone. The framework has five questions. Thanks to the United Nations, we have 17 sustainable development goals. (Sometimes there is talk of adding one or two more.) Despite the fact that most people think about them as 17 independent issues, in truth they are an interdependent ecosystem. Attempts to demonstrate the SDGs as a systems challenge have resulted in complicated feedback loop diagrams and systems impact calculations and indices. Somehow, I don't see the average planning officer in any small island developing state doing this. In fact, even in WEIRD countries, the average beleaguered bureaucrat does not have the bandwidth to take on learning these complex system design tools, even though they make beautiful pictures.

These five principles – the principle of Sustainable Systems; the principle of Meaningful Moral metrics; the principle of Anticipatory Agency; the principle of Robust Resilience; the principle of Transformational Technology can improve the teleologically effective design of any project, program, or policy design and analysis. We will go through each of the five principles below to introduce you to the SMART Futures Framework.

The Principle of Sustainable Systems

The first principle is to ask the question "How is this (Policy? Program? Project?) I am designing a Sustainable System?" And, as needed, further refine to address how the system is sustainable over its life cycle. Be it a [fill in the blank] oil and gas project or hospital complex or water main replacement and so on. Given that some capital investment projects have 40-year life cycles, how are you ensuring that your design process explores what forty years hence looks like? This question ensures that the stakeholders in the design process recognize that both the problem space and the solutions space are systems, and that they are interrelated. All stakeholders have a thread of the problem that is important to the weaving of the resolution. If I apply this metaphor to advancing health care for all, we need the thread of access to medicines, the thread of access to insurance, the thread of access to water and sanitation, to public education, and so on, to shaping a teleologically effective response. The challenge is that quite often, these issues are in different ministries or departments, and so the bureaucratic devil of protocolary (or customs of the bureaucracy) delay dance begins. This is the pebble in the shoe as we journey to better decision-making. Our governance structures are too often obstacles to the solutions we seek. Too many ascribe scientific law to economics and development planning, when in fact, it is a social science and thus in large part – a form of art. I say this, knowing that many will now call me a heretic, but if we are to speak truth to power, we must acknowledge that there are many known unknowns that we cannot define by a neat mathematical equation or sexy graph. Some of the things that we need to fix cannot be measured by the metrics at hand and indeed may not be quantifiable at all. It frightens me to see how much more excited we get at headlines that cite research to replace our missing bees with artificial drone insect pollinating machines than we get for proposals to replace the real bees we have lost, and/or regenerate systems that induce the natural bees back to their former state of thriving. As if drone bees are going to be healthfully sustainable for the environment. Asking this Sustainable System question first opens the door to a set of follow-on questions. The systems question is the same whether you are an engineer, a lawyer, a policymaker, a healthcare specialist, or an information technology (IT) expert. Your job title or function makes no difference to the question. It is how you answer that question that creates the deflection points in the design process.

I want to stop to breathe here, and I invite you to take that in. Because what I am saying is so simple that it may sound naïve. I can hear the skeptic in you asking, "Can a simple question begin a paradigm shift?" And I say unquestionably, "Yes." All scientific inquiry begins with a question. Why is the sky blue? How are corals formed? What if we had drought for seven years? Our passion for the pursuit of answers drives human innovation. If we want to create a sustainable world, we have to – all of us no matter what we are designing — ask that fundamental question, "Is this sustainable?" as a starting point to leading us to our preferred destination.

The Principle of Meaningful Metrics

"What does it mean to be sustainable?" might lead to "Sustainable to serve whom?" This is the heart of the principle of meaningful and moral metrics. We all know the saying "we measure what we value." As such, when we think about the fact that all systems are created on the basis of some metric, we must ask if these are meaningful and moral metrics. It is important to weight the word "meaningful" with the notion of "moral" because in some cases there might be a meaningful metric that leads to undesirable outcomes for those not in the power seat. The stories of King Herod and Hitler stand as testimony to that fact. They achieved their metrics, but to what end? We must ask the question, "How do we measure what matters in our global march to sustainability?" How do we define and ensure meaningful moral metrics? Metrics based on the moral law that says first, do no harm. This allows us to look at first, second and third order impacts more effectively. Whether we are talking about how we mine the Earth, how we use Outer Space, how we treat water, or how we educate children, we need to ask how to do it with ethics and meaningful metrics. This question does not offer any preset rules as what said metrics must be. The goal of this question is to interrogate the status quo rulebooks and move us away from standards and measures that no longer serve us.

Let's take the case of education and school. We want all children in school, and our standard is that children should spend six hours in school a day. For years we have known that the education system was failing many children, for a variety of reasons. Because some children do better with the morning, and some do better with the afternoon because of their biorhythms. Because children have different learning styles –

kinetic, auditory, visual, tactile. Because children have varying attention spans, and so on. The conversation about designing an educational system for the twenty-first century has been raging for some time. It is no secret that we don't need schools to operate like factories anymore. We need children with critical thinking, educated to be able to work alongside robots and artificial intelligence (AI). We want them to be able to problem-solve, think ahead, and dream big dreams to solve the problems they will inherit. Yet, we have been unable to make the systems change. That is until now. Until the COVIDemic came and forced us into digital hibernation. Now we are forced to make haste to design metrics to make this shift in such a way as to mitigate against the digital divide creating new forms of exclusion.

We know that we need to do away with the Gospel of Growth according to the Gross Domestic Product (GDP). The GDP is not a moral metric. Metrics like the Human Development Index and inequality coefficients and vulnerability, sustainability and happiness indices that people are trying to push, have not really ascended to the high altar of global governance, but they bring into being more Meaningful and Moral Metrics to the lives of humans. There is an elephant in the room in every design process. How do we measure sustainability, impact, effectiveness of programs, return on investment? How do we measure disempowerment, inequality, inequity, discrimination? We are still in the thrall of economic mindsets and equations which may no longer apply.

As we deepen our travail in the thickets of the fourth Industrial Revolution, the economic and scientific laws that accompany AI, blockchain, cryptocurrency, and internet of things, robotics, neurotech, biotech and a host of other technological shifts are challenging the way we do business. If we want to move to a circular or regenerative economy, because now that we know there is no such thing as a free lunch or a place called away, we need to account for waste disposal and other costs to the common of our good life. And by the way, this includes us thinking about the cost of removal of Space debris in pricing of the Space economy.

A few cities and countries are beginning experiments with wellbeing as a metric. Will it take on in the post-COVID world? That is left to be seen, but there are seeds of change on the way as take note of how Gen X and Gen Z are really concerned with quality of life and less so about consumption and growth. This explains the swift uptake of the sharing economy, i.e., the Uber-fication of "low use goods" that you only use for a short time. Indeed, despite COVID-19, and possible setbacks, I believe there will soon be devices and cleaners invented to sanitize, just so the sharing economy can flourish. It is worthwhile to observe the seeds of change happening in Wales, Scotland, and Nepal such as the gross national happiness index, and explore means by which we can spread these ideas. For there lies the way of the future. This is not to say we are going to completely replace all the metrics that we have now. It is to say, we must always identify best moral metric fit to the problem at hand. Because in speaking of healthcare, all the metrics that matter in India may not be the same metrics that have meaning in the Caribbean. Obviously, the rules of global governance require common metrics for information sharing and metrics that can cross the borders, even if we agree that no one measure fits all boats.

The COVIDemic and the after-effects have added to countries' economic burden of debt. Now is as good a time as any for the High Court organization of the IMF, World Bank, and the Regional Development Banks to convene a working group on meaningful moral metrics. This is needed especially for small island development states (SIDS), that have been crying out for some time about the inherent bias when an island the size of a matchstick is judged against a country the size of a yard stick. The second principle – addressed in the question, "do we have meaningful moral metrics that measure what matters?"

The Third Principle of Anticipatory Agency

The concept of agency comes from the idea that in every system there are stakeholders, and each stakeholder has their own agency. That is, each agent has the ability to pursue their own goals, whether we're talking about the agent in an organization, in a nation, in a city. Often in the design process we forget the agency of the stakeholders in the system to impact the efficacy of the proposed solution. In designing policies, programs or projects, the level of power of the stakeholders or agents in the system determines their ability to impact the design process. More often than not, power is distributed between the public and private sector. Indeed, in the dominant model of marketplace capitalism, the corporation seems to have emerged as the most powerful social agent, working hand in hand with government to create the laws that benefit their interests first and foremost. Then, the appropriate environmental and social safeguards are applied to mitigate the probable harm. This dynamic is the prevailing order in our problem-solving ecosystem. If the situation is handled well, the plural sector puts up a fight to change the process or protocols and most times we find that the process is too far along to be stopped. The best we can hope for in that system is "do less harm." The ability of corporations to function with rights of citizenship changed the ecosystem in such a way that it has led to indigenous people using these arguments to move to establishing personhood for nature. We see seeds of this change in Bolivia, Ecuador and New Zealand where laws have been passed to protect nature: that is a river and a mountain have been given personhood.

This principle is put into practice through the question, "how does the design of this system promote or benefit from Anticipatory Agency of the stakeholders?" This might lead to a follow-on question such as "how might stakeholder agency impact successful operations over the life cycle of the system?" Or "how might we anticipate a design to help shape the adaptability and agility of the agents?" Given that we know we are in a period of rapid change, how might the agency of each stakeholder be reflected in the design? Modelling of social network analysis and/or agency network analysis is a complex process. What is important is asking the question to understand the role of the stakeholders and their agency as we think about the problem we are addressing. The answer to this open-ended question will normally bring to the surface key leverage points in the system. This question by itself will not necessarily dilute the dominant power structures. What the question provides is a more accurate picture of the system under study, and thus the possibility of an improvement in the design for optimal impact, where optimal means something more than a satisfactory economic return on investment. This question and its aftermath bring into focus all the stakeholder agents in the system, and provides opportunity for identifying root cause.

The Fourth Principle of Robust Resilience

In this era of the disaster news cycles, be it hurricanes, flash floods, tornadoes, forest fires and/or earthquakes, the word resilience has entered common usage. In general, it means to bounce back whether we are talking about physical resilience, mental resilience, emotional resilience, or social resilience. Resilience is about being resilient against, or to something. So, resilience is about addressing any perceived threats or vulnerabilities of the system which you are designing. The question that could be put as follows: "How are we designing for Robust Resilience?" That is, of the people, and the processes in the system we are designing.

Let us look at physical resilience, and the context of cyber-attacks in the central banking world. In this instance, will have to look at the hardware, the software as well as the humans running the system, that is, all of the agents in the systems, and ask and answer the question, have we designed the information systems of the central banks of the world to be resilient to potential shocks – man-made hacks and/or natural disasters? The same resilience question could be asked of a transportation system in a city. Is the metro system resilient for a flood, given the city is prone to flash floods and now with rising sea levels – bearing in mind the experience of Hurricane Harvey and the New York Metro system? What about smart cities and self-driving cars in the event of a power grid outage? What is the resilience for power-failure-induced smart car traffic congestion? Despite the desire to control the weather, hurricanes, tornados, storms, floods and the once a century solar flare, power systems failure is still a potential hazard.

In respect to social resilience, the 2020 COVIDemic is a global field experiment in social resilience. We find many people underinsured or uninsured now addressing catastrophic financial challenges because their out-of-pocket health care expenses cannot be met by the savings they have. How will the financial system respond to this unpaid debt? How will the health care system evolve to ensure lack of funds by some does not preclude access to treatment and thus create undue harm to others. Anticipatory Agency and its fraternal twin siblings – agility and adaptability – ensures that we design for best response to both known knowns and known unknowns, and a state of well-informed preparedness or Robust Resilience.

Designing for resilience demands that we design from a lens of addressing the question what could happen, that is designing to prevent, withstand or mitigate against those unwanted things that could happen. Another way to look at the issue of resilience, to think about it again from an engineering perspective, is: what about recovery? How soon can you restore the system to normalcy? We have heard the question a lot regarding the COVIDemic. When will we get back to normal? How will we recover going back to work? Well, it's not as easy as changing a light bulb or putting in switches that blew up because of a storm. Because you're talking about a virus which could morph anytime. You're talking about people that have different capabilities to withstand, at the personal level, the disease. This question is part of the design process. This is why engineers, the military, and soccer/football teams spend so much time in simulating plays. Another question might be how do we create a resilience function that can evolve with the system's evolution? Because in truth social problems are, more often than not, dynamic. We have learned some things from the 2020 pandemic about public health rules-making in the age of the internet that hopefully prepares us to better manage the arc of future hazards of the same kind.

A resilience mindset demands a wide-angled view of the system and a transdisciplinary approach. Because, no matter how hard we try, we, each of us, have a bias that carries blinders. In looking at the US public health system, the engineer, the nurse and the lawyer each see different problems. This is why we need to be comfortable with interdependent thinking. SMART Futures design demands the inclusion of all stakeholder viewpoints in the system by thoroughly addressing the "who is in the room and who is affected" question. Successful resilience design requires that we see the inter-relationship of the whole as well as the parts. We all need air, water and food. And we know the order and the relationship based on the time to expiration if we don't have them: air, then water, then food. But the fact is we will need them all to survive. Usually, in the engineered environment, we measure the cost of building the safety feature in against the trade-off of not doing it. This is why so much is spent on making sure that nuclear energy plants have Robust Resilience. We don't do that in the social world where the use of the term resilience has become jargonized and, in some ways, has caused us to normalize some of the unwanted things that are happening around us. People need to be resilient to the systems instead of the systems being resilient for the people.

And starting now, we must design and build for resilience that also includes, as a part of the system, nature itself. We have treated water and soil and the forest and the sea as exogenous variables. That is why we have not taken account of the management of our waste stream in the profit and loss equations. We can no longer separate resilience planning from building for sustainability. We already know that based on science, we're going to have more flooding in the next ten years. Even with the best of intentions to reduce carbon emissions, we cannot put the climate change genie back in the bottle. We have observed hundreds of thousands of acres of forest being burnt around the world: Australia, Brazil, California. We have seen the extinction of many species. We have seen flooding in West Africa and Asia. Already, we have forced movements of people due to weather events. Nature would eventually repair itself without us. Yet, we are still here doing the same thing ad nauseum, and, to the extent that whatever we're doing now in the name of development – be it a cobalt mine, be it a power company, an oil well, cutting down forests for paper – whatever it is we no longer have the luxury of being ignorant, or pretending to be blind to the reality that we have observed. This for me, is the gift hidden in the crisis of the COVIDemic. Because no one is 100 percent sure that they are truly safe. Never mind the anti-mask-wearing live free or die survivalists. They, too, know well that things and times have changed. And we know that the probability of the advent of more pandemics within the coming hundred years is significantly high for the twenty-first century because of the decimation of huge areas of forests, which have reduced habitat from the animals and the insects that need forests to survive, and thus reduced the habitat of the millions of uncharted viruses. Robust Resilience in design must therefore resonate with a long-term perspective.

The Principle of the Transformational Use of Technology

The fifth principle is the transformational use of technology. We live in an Industry 4.0 world. This brings both promise and peril. The transformational use of technology implies the designer has choice to assess how technology might best serve the problem situation. The question to be asked here is, "How might we 'transformationally' use technology to drive achievement of the desired outcome?" A key challenge in policy, program or project design is often the lack of technology impact assessment that helps anticipate the second, and third order impacts. The goal is to design such that: 1) technology is an enabling agent for us to have a better outcome; and 2) the technology's potential negative impacts are minimized or mitigated. We are fully aware that the fast rate of technological change has outstripped the ability of our judicial, legal, and regulatory institutions to keep up. This has left room for misuse, ill-use and abuse of technology. The tension between promise and peril must be managed. With artificial intelligence (AI), we can get apps that use Space and satellite data to support our needs for weather data, water management, precision agriculture, and GPS for finding our way in the world. The same AI could probably be used for face recognition, which might end up with people being mistakenly identified, or in the case of contact tracing Apps for the COVIDemic, used to inhibit free speech, civil society organizing and political dissidence. The onus will be on the project designers as always to make sure that technology applications of interest actually can create a transformational shift to the better for the design challenge.

The promise of technology to provide abundance is well accepted. The case of the mobile phone in Africa which has allowed many to leapfrog stages of technology adoption is often touted. But whether we are talking about smartphones, 3D printing, biotechnology, nanotechnology, internet of things,

5G and 6G on the drawing boards, augmented or virtual reality, or any of the other technologies driving change, the issue in each situation is to ensure that we don't create new problems by solving old problems. We want to ensure that we do not overlook any second and third order impacts of a new technology in an ecosystem by asking the question explicitly. This is really a critical time in our global decision-making. There is a lot of innovation happening even in the emerging economies. One wrong move and we trip ourselves into self-extinction.

What this question about transformational technology does is put on the table the question of the potential role of innovation in both the problem and solution space. There is a techno-hypnotic high that is driving change. Besides the ongoing battle for supremacy of one nation over another, there is the unholy rush to be the first and to be seen to be a winner. Techno-narcissism combined with the power of AI, is loosening the boundaries of moral science. The fact that laws and policies are lagging behind the rate of technology emergence means that there is more responsibility for self-policing and voluntary guidelines on the part of the academic and private sector to curtail their impulses to rush in where angels fear to tread. Frankenstein and other science fiction dystopias should serve as cautionary tales that help us to see beyond our biases. We have to call into being, or midwife this new way of thinking so that scientific researchers and industry associations add this lens to their policing of themselves. Asking the question, "How might this technology I am so excited about designing create more problems than it solves?" and then design a solution to mitigate that.

We can fly halfway around the world in fifteen hours. We have technologies that allow us to listen to someone speak in one language and see or hear the translation in our language. We have technologies that allowed us to put in place protocols for rapid testing for the COVIDemic which has improved and increased testing capabilities in much shorter times than ever before. And this is all good. But we also have to face the fact that in doing this we have created a new set of problems. We need to do a better job of designing for transformational or at the least beneficial impact. This is most likely why many technology designers are using biomimicry as a framing for their design processes. We could learn a lot from the questions biomimicry asks, because they are both transformational and systemic.

Bringing the Principles Together

These five principles go together like the fingers on a hand. The questions are mutually reinforcing. In every design instance the problem at hand will dictate the weight and direction of the solution process but we cannot say that the design principles around metrics and resilience are more important than those around agency or transformative use of technology. All five are necessary and with all of them come sufficient questions to help us all become more effective at resolving the complex challenges of systems of systems problems. The sweeping transformation envisioned by the 17 sustainable development goals requires achieving numerous unspecified changes in access to information and communication technology and space in which they are enmeshed. These five principles support anyone, at any level, ordering their thoughts to secure buy-in from the relevant stakeholders. The narrative of systems thinking must be placed front and center if we are to enable the development of critical thinking needed to address the complexity of the challenges we are facing. Everything is Everything. We cannot pursue health care if we don't pursue access to clean water and sanitation. In the same way you cannot pursue Moral Metrics but not pursue Robust Resilience. We must recognize that the boundaries we put on a problem space are there because of the economic decision of time and effort that we make so as to manage ourselves as well as the system. But we must remain mindful that at the quantum level there is no boundary.

We need SMART Futures thinking across all sectors and systems. We need for educators and engineers and evangelists to become part of the sustainability movement by ensuring that they put on the mind of "Providentia" – the muse of providence – and get SMART about the future they are designing. This critical thinking style is needed by everyone no matter the point of entry – lawyer, doctor or police chief.

Sharing stories is a very powerful way to elicit behavior change. The rehearsal of the future that we undertake in using this SMART Futures framework for sustainability design is our preparation for shaping that future. We do not need an authority to begin to work with the SMART Futures Framework. There is no need for me to trademark the process or require certification in the use of this framework in order for anyone to use it. This framework embodies three ethical principles. Democracy of Power. Democracy of Design. Democracy of the Future.

We do not have the luxury of four hundred years to save ourselves. There is fierce urgency to become more adept at global "solutioneering." The pregnant pause caused by the COVIDemic provided us an unprecedented opportunity to rebirth the future. As Tolstoy said, "Everyone thinks of changing the world, but no one thinks of changing himself." What we need is not another set of SDGs or extending the time to reach the goals or change the values in the goals. What we need is to change our minds. We need to have a shared philosophy of sustainability, and a shared language of how to solve complex problems across transdisciplinary borders. The SMART Futures Framework uses five effective questions to access ways to reset our minds and so reset the future.

Day Six
The Year 2035
Anansi Took a Dive into 2035

ReSources: A Global News Service about Renewable Energy
July 4, 2035, UN International Day of Cooperatives

*Finland's announcement that it has met its target to achieve carbon
neutrality by 2035 has been met with worldwide acclaim. They are
among the top 20 countries, including Korea, Ghana, Barbados and
Fiji, in the world that have met this target. It would seem as if the
small island developing states are leading the way. This feat was
accomplished through a combination of policies that shifted increased
investment in renewable energies across the board. Globally, since
2025, solar energy technologies have had the most dramatic impact on
reducing carbon emissions, but unfortunately, this has also increased
potential risks for cadmium poisoning. Cadmium poisoning has been
reported from many parts of the world. Long-term exposure to cadmium
(measurable in the blood, urine, hair, nail and saliva samples) through
air, water, soil, and food leads to cancer and organ system toxicity.
In this year's Annual meeting of the International Renewable Energy
Agency (IRENA), the International Renewable Energy Cooperative
(IREC) will run a one-day workshop for stakeholders to experience
simulation of the life of a solar panel. The goal of this simulation is to
bring education and awareness of the second and third order impacts
of the solar waste challenges in the hopes of preparing the participants
to better understand what is at stake for humanity, if recycling policies
and processes are not put in place now. It is estimated that at current
rate of use of the panels, there would be 60 million tons of photovoltaic
(PV) panels waste lying in landfills by the year 2050. IREC has been
working hand in hand with the International Society for Regenerative
Economics (ISRE) founded in the wake of the COVID-19 pandemic
which estimates that failure to recycle will cost millions as states
and the industry are forced to pay lawsuits in the billions. These*

lawsuits are being brought by the Just Futures Coalition, now present in approximately 50 countries, which has filed a series of landmark lawsuits against countries, corporations, and cities for crimes against nature, or crimes against future generations. Such crimes include operating without recycling or regeneration policies and plans. Currently, almost 95% of glass and 85% of the silicon material can be recycled. The simulation program was designed and built by Ubuntu Arcades, a gaming design company which aims to promote improved policy decision support for complex systems of systems challenges. This news comes amidst the sobering news that the temperature rise trends are still hovering above the desired 1.5C as the island nation of the Bahamas reports the decision to resettle over 15,000 people from three of their Out Islands to the new capital on Abaco. Coming up in our good news feature, we report on IREC's progress with harnessing solar energy from space, as well as improving ocean energy powered air conditioning systems.

Chapter 6

How Do We Make the Shift?

How can we foster the birth of this new story of being and thriving in the world? We agree that new ways of thinking are needed to create global sustainability. We understand at the core, clearing the hornets' nest is about reframing the problems and their root cause by seeing them as systems of systems. Thus, the need for an emergent design approach, as dynamic as the problem space which can be best executed as five questions about the future.

1. How might we address the solution as a Sustainable System?
2. How might we design using Meaningful Metrics?
3. How do we design solutions that enable Anticipatory and adaptive Agency of all stakeholders?
4. How might the design process achieve Robust Resilience of all parts of the system – live and manmade?
5. How can we incorporate Transformational Technology for the greater good?

In the last 50 years of global architecting, we have lived through the green movement, the gender movement, indigenous people's movement, the equity and inclusion agenda against discrimination of all types – disabilities, stigma for HIV AIDS for LGBTQ. We have had short-lived bursts such as the "50 Years Is Enough" moment and the "Occupy Wall Street" moment which came, did some good, but did not take root. These days we see more and more movements colliding (if not coalescing) around common challenges like climate change, even as there remains a North-South and racial divide. The most recent manifestation of global foment is the Black Lives Matter uprising. However, we know from the Arab Spring experience, street protests may not always converge to a long-term path to sustainable solutions.

A movement is not just a three-day or three-week or event three-month protest. It takes a long-term, steady, sustained effort to achieve meaningful, long-term, sustained change. We know that these protests are signs that people are hungry for change and willing to take to the streets. It's important for us to figure out how we might benefit from the current disgruntled populace who have lost faith in politics, or "politricks," but still have some faith in themselves and people. How might we create the conditions for a paradigm shift in reality? A paradigm shift will not happen by simply addressing the surface litany of problems, we have to go to root cause, and we have to get to tipping point. It takes breaking an old habit and forming new ones.

The theory of change I'm using is based on a 2011 Rensselaer Polytechnic Study that stated that when 10% of a country or community believe that a fringe idea makes sense or can become the norm, it then has the ability to become a new norm. Sustainability is no longer a fringe idea. It is everyone's business. The whole world. We want to build a long-term movement that includes people who are operating at any level, anywhere, whether they are corporate employees or small business employees or small business owners; whether they are members of the Girl Scouts or the Rotary Club; whether they are in politics or public service. Thus, the focus of my approach to creating the conditions for a paradigm shift to SMART Futures is to focus on "WE the People" who already see ourselves as connected to, or active in, the cause of sustainability, even if not actively engaged in any "official movement" or UN SDGS program or project. When we secure opportunities to get enough people to apply the SMART Futures thinking framework, it becomes the new normal way of thinking about problem-solving and policy, program or project design. Thus, at the very least, we will have to get at least ten percent of people engaged in the UN SDGs using this framework. We will also have to try to get the SMART Futures framework to be used by ten percent of the people who already believe themselves to be part of the sustainability conversation but who are outside the traditional sustainable development circles. The challenge is to find a way to link all the different threads of the system of systems, in such a way as to bring us all into the same litany and the same mythology. The SMART Futures lens could accomplish this.

For global sustainability we would need almost one billion people, that is about ten percent of the world. How do we get to one million people? Or even one hundred thousand? How do we build this movement? Protests fizzle out and die, and paradigm shifts don't make for can't miss TV headline news. But right now, we are in a seminal moment. The COVIDemic has provided us a global strategic infection point. Global consciousness, the capacity and disposition to understand and act upon issues of global significance is at a high state of resonance. This is a decisive moment that marks the start of significant change. The global architecture must respond to disruptive change in the environment effectively or face deterioration. Most of the world including those of us who see ourselves as both a global actor and member of a local community — be it a city or a state or a nation — capable of making a positive contribution to the world are faced with making choices.

People are looking for answers to what should be done to reset our vision. We have a unique opportunity to breach boundary walls, cross borders to tear down silos to make the connections across "-isms" and weave an interconnected tapestry of the future we want. Anybody anywhere can use these five principles and ask these five questions to address their specific design of the future challenge.

We need an evolutionary shift of global consciousness in

the direction of shared stewardship for Earth. We need to set intentions, which has been proven to change outcomes. The discovery of quantum physics has proven the interconnected nature of reality in scientific experiments. This gives context to Pierre Teilhard de Chardin's construct of the noosphere, which in short brings into focus, the idea of a sort of "biosphere of ideas" in which human reason and thoughts exist. Just as there is a biosphere of plants and animals, and bacteria and viruses, the noosphere is the sphere where ideas and concepts live. The noosphere is about the collective consciousness of ideas, the shared beliefs, moral attitudes, mythologies of humanity.

You might dismiss it as nonsense, but the fun part is you don't need to believe it. We come together when there is an Olympics or FIFA World Cup; this resonance has been mapped and measured. The biggest resonances happen for traumatic events, like when Princess Diana died. I was not surprised to read the science on this because much to my surprise, I found myself glued to the television weeping copious tears; even though I would not describe myself as a royal watcher or heavy television watcher in any sense of the word beforehand. Yet there I was stuck in the news loop for a good 12 hours. I believe we are at a similar point of global resonance around the grief and fear we feel, and the search for the right question and direction forward. For many people, it's been a moment not just of reflection but also of gestation as people scramble to design the return to normal as part of their coping mechanism for the high level of uncertainty we are living through. To benefit from the opportunity of this seminal moment, to give birth to this paradigm shift, we need a shared language and framework.

The SMART Futures framework offers a universally applicable lens for problem-solving, using the form of five guiding questions. This approach creates a shared language across different sectors of interest and helps to build coherence and resonance. The fact is we are accustomed to the idea of smart technology in the form of smartphones, cars, homes, smart money, smart government that allows us to do all our government services online, so much so that we sometimes seem to forget that being human is more than a unit of consumption and/or production and human flourishing means more than a series of efficient transactions. Given that near 4 billion people carry a smartphone, it is my belief that adopting the word SMART to describe the approach will benefit from the global consciousness inherent in the term. The fact is, even if we don't know why our personal digital assistants are called smart, and we don't know how they work, we use them for almost everything. Similarly, there is no need for the user to understand the scientific and psychological principles explained in order to benefit from asking these five questions. It is enough to simply use them as a framework when doing policy, program or project design for sustainability. The use of the term "futures" is a deliberate choice to signal that there is no single shared vision of the future. Each of the 7.8 billion of us on the planet carries many visions of the future in the cone of possibility. Yet what we want has converged in the form of the SDGs which outline statistics that define a more equitable life and opportunities to flourish now. We want to address how we share our planet, our rules book, our decision-making, our humanity in such a way as to arrive at global sustainability.

A Global Meshwork of Labs of Labs

To launch this movement, I propose seeding a Global Collaboratory or global lab of labs meshwork aimed at addressing collective conscious problem-solving. This concept builds off a proposal that was explored at a Salzburg Seminar on the Future in spring, 2018. To test the efficacy of this "Global Collaboratory" construct, which is to promote shared language and shared vision, I am proposing to explore four of the SDGs, that is four experiments over the next ten years in four 30-month legs of a relay to the year 2030. The Global Collaboratory will pilot four participatory processes focused on zero hunger (SDG 2), water and sanitation (SDG 8), education (SDG 4), and health (SDG 6) and will be chartered by networks from the public sector (Leader Tribe); the private sector (Merchant Tribe); the education sector (the Mentor Tribe); the plural sector (Caretaker Tribe) respectively. The media and entertainment sector (Talebearer Tribe) would be included as a partner in each of the labs. All the labs would be constituted through a network of at least thirty participating countries (representing a little over ten percent of countries in the United Nations). Each design lab in each country would be organized around a participatory planning process adopting the SMART Futures Framework convened by an already proven influencer or thought Leader.

The Way of the Leader Tribe

The Global Collaboratory to be undertaken through a network of public sector organizations is SDG 2, or Zero Hunger, which has as its first target, "By 2030, end hunger and ensure access by all people, in particular the poor and people in vulnerable situations, including infants, to safe, nutritious and sufficient food all year round." A big agenda, the targets address issues relevant to farming the future from maintaining the genetic diversity of seeds, cultivated plants and farmed and domesticated animals and their related wild species, to increasing investment, including through enhanced international cooperation, in rural infrastructure, agricultural research and extension services, technology development and plant and livestock gene banks in order to enhance agricultural productive capacity in developing countries, in particular least developed countries. This lab would be convened by governments from 30 countries. In every country/government the different government agencies that address the issues related to the food/hunger nexus in their country would be part of the SDG Design lab, for example, fisheries, farming, forestry, climate, hydrology, agriculture finance, soil science and the list goes on considering the entire value chain of what is needed to create food security. There is a different vocabulary and metrics for problem-solving for each of these subsectors and oftentimes there seems to be conflicting interests. The aim of each national lab would be to convene whole systems design explorations for series of polices, programs and projects that would result in achieving SDG 2 for that country. All stakeholders in the system under study would be invited to participate in SMART Futures conversations and design labs based on the 2030 goals. Given we are addressing the issue of food, which might include global commodities, this could necessitate inclusion of international organizations with responsibility for international rules and regulations that govern issues from pesticide use and management to food processing safety guidelines. The guiding question would be, "What might we do to ensure we have met the goals of Ending Hunger by 2030 and accelerate achievement of the SDG 2?" Imagine 30 countries undertaking this process from the poorest to the middle income but highly vulnerable countries. Imagine a Global Collaboratory that links these labs into a free-flowing exchange of information about various policy or technical or social challenges, and technical solutions tried and the outcomes. Decisions as to specific tools and metrics will be made at the national level in keeping with both local laws and norms as well as aspirations. The act of collaboration and exchange will reduce knowledge gaps and mishaps and support the creation of a shared vision for the SDG 2 intention. This global consciousness is beginning to take place owing to increasing public awareness of the die-off of bees and what it could mean for our food supplies in the future. By using the

SMART Futures framework to create a shared thought-field for people to work together in search of SDG 2, we're creating a highly cohesive, and coherent field in which the likelihood of approaching resonance and the intended goal is higher. In this Collaboratory, the leading government agency, which presumably has convening power, would be responsible for arranging the design rules and processes and reporting on outputs and outcomes over the life of the relay to 2030.

The Way of the Merchant Tribe

The second Global Collaboratory will be chartered by the Private Sector or Merchant Tribe. The Lab we will begin with is SDG 6, that is: "Ensure access to water and sanitation for all, that is to say by 2030 achieve universal and equitable access to safe and affordable drinking water for all." We already have a lot of people concerned with the issue of water as studies show that by 2040 we will be a water stressed world. What if the Merchants active in the water sector in a given country that is, the companies processing chemicals, or food or energy for power, or just plain bottled water –were to come together run a design lab to address water challenges collectively in their country? Now imagine a Global Collaboratory in which water futures design labs are run in thirty (30) of the most water-stressed countries convened to address the challenge question, "How might we best achieve SDG 6?" The countries should reflect the diversity of the issues ranging from island nations like Barbados to countries in the Middle East to a country like South Africa, which already experienced severe water stress, to the US which is also experiencing high water stress in states like California. The lab would engage all stakeholders in the system. The SMART Futures framework would be applied across transdisciplinary boundaries that define the diversity of science, engineering and technology futures that are driving changes in the sector in addition to impacting social issues.

Sub-questions that might arise, based on the given situation, might include assuring the efficient use of water, or returning the water they use back to the planet as clean or even cleaner than when they first got it.

Now imagine labs in 30 different countries, from every stakeholder clan in their water system — climatologists, hydrologists, regulators, scientists, engineers, policymakers — anybody that has any knowledge about how water is used, including the everyday people interested in promoting something like a virtuous cycle of water.

In using the SMART Futures framework, they would enter the process by asking, "What does a Sustainable System look like in 2030?" They would explore and define Meaningful Metrics for water in their national context. Without damaging others in the first do-no-harm moral law of metrics we value. What might affordable access to water look like in 2030? Who will have agency in this system and how anticipatory and adaptive will both agents and the system be? What should be done to ensure Robust Resilience? For each country, this might look different. In terms of resilience, in country X, they would have to deal with floods; in country Y, the issue might be drought; or in country Z, sea level rise or it might be that in one country all challenges apply. Finally, what are the Transformative ways in which Technology can be harnessed to improve efficiencies of collection, measuring, distributing, cleaning, all the different elements that you think you can improve in the management of water. Each country design lab is then curated in a global meshwork – a lab of labs which allows for free sharing and exchanging of the knowledge that they are gaining. Nobody wins when one country or company is starved of water. Because it creates instability in one part of the system, and therefore it creates instability throughout the whole system. Rather than prognosticating on the future of war being equivalent to the future of water, let the Merchant Tribes loose to innovate solutions that meet the UN Agenda 2030 and observe the shifts happen.

The Way of the Mentor Tribe

What might be the role of the education sector in helping to promote the SMART Futures paradigm? This SMART Futures paradigm needs to be taught in schools, that is a definite part of creating critical thinkers and problem-solvers. However, it might be useful to work to solve a real-world problem such as SDG 4 on Education, which aims to "ensure inclusive and equitable quality education and promote lifelong learning opportunities for all" and is made up of 10 targets.

The Global Collaboratory would be convened by a network of universities from 30 countries around the world that already have pledged support to the sustainable development goals. Given the targets, the design process in each country would begin with an interrogation of the future for education of education for 2030 in terms of policies, programs and/or project design that could result in desired outcomes especially given the programmatic discussions being held in the corridors of the international financial institutions. Again, the labs would consist of a transdisciplinary team that is involved in all stages of the design lifecycle for life-long education.

Certainly, the lab would include the participation of K-12 stakeholders in the design process for many of us know first-hand the "precocious" acuity of today's five-year-old preschooler who will be seeing their terrible teens in 2030. As digital natives, it is important to design solutions that take into account their facility with the screen and thus opportunities to develop new metrics, Robust Resilience and to apply transformative uses of technology that affirms learning. That's the way of the Mentor.

The Way of the Caretaker Tribe

How might the plural sector of civil society play a leading role in the Global Collaboratory process? Up until now they have been a supporting role in the various labs. Their responsibility was to show up when asked as opposed to taking the lead. NGOs tend to be people who self-organize an issue of their choice. Some of them are rebels, some are daredevils, some are doers, all are Caretakers. Whether this be for professional or personal reasons, the point is they are organized around causes that most usually are in sync with the UN SDGs. The Caretakers run the gamut from social-issue-cause activists to environmental NGOs, to professional associations. But at the root, they are all doing the same thing: taking care of an issue or sector they are interested in. There is a Caretaker group for every issue in the SDGs.

Part of the challenge is that each "-ism" has its own rules and regulations and lingua franca. As an aside, what I find fascinating is that sometimes the "-ism" doesn't even have a shared language to describe what they are fighting for. Take the anti-racism movement, what is it fighting for? One cannot say "I want an anti-racist future." What is the opposite of racist or racism? There does not seem to be a word, at least an English word, that defines what it is we want. That might very well be one of the reasons we are having such a hard time getting there. How can you create that which you cannot fully define? I have tried without success to interject the word "humanitism" as an antidote. Back to the main point.

As a unifying issue we could take SDG 3. Ensure healthy lives and promote wellbeing for all at all ages. Everybody wants a healthy life – especially now. Whether or not you're fighting for gender rights, or prison reform, or affordable clean energy, or climate change or sustainable inclusive growth and living wage and decent work; health impacts on you personally. What if civil society in 30 countries decided to organize a Global Collaboratory on the issue of SDG 3?

In this Global Collaboratory, at the national level, NGOs

could self-organize consultations on health care futures. In this lab, different NGOs who normally would not work on the same issue, would come together over health care because it affects them all. Using the trans disciplinary approach that the SMART Futures framework proposes, members of plural civil society from the faith community to the labor union movement to professional associations to NGOs representing the Merchant Tribes. All stakeholders would be convened by NGO healthcare and wellbeing advocates. The 30 national labs would be convened as a lab of labs to permit cross fertilization and hybridization of design, and then mapping for comparative assessment across 30 countries at the same time.

The countries would self-select among these first four global collabs. Countries that are at war would not be allowed to participate. In each Global Collaboratory, care would be taken to ensure fairly even continental participation among the developing countries.

The Way of the Talebearer Tribe

What role for media and entertainment? We are so distracted by the 24/7 news and entertainment cycle that we are not paying attention to critical matters. The Talebearers bear some culpability for our inability to see the crisis we are in for what it is. They are critical to the formation of planetary or global consciousness which includes both a sensitivity to local phenomena and experiences as manifestations of broader developments on the planet as well as the capacity to think and act in informed ways about issues of both global and local significance. The Talebearers should educate the average "every-person" about how to play their part in bringing forth the paradigm shift to a new norm in reference to sustainability. There was a season when pop songs about social problems were common. These days we find a narcissistic worldview of self and clique idolatry, gangster rap and prosperity gospel in the thesis of our music. We have popular music singing endless ditties about unrequited love and/or flashy cars, and anthems to self-love utilizing saccharine electronically measured soundtracks and a plethora of dystopian movies about the future but relatively few that carry a tale of an aspirational view of what a future could look like. Dystopian movies play to our limbic mind which seems to get a thrill from being terrorized. We pay to experience terror. We go on roller coasters and scream our lungs out, come off shaking and then pay and go back again. Not me. I was cured after the first ride. I don't find any joy in being terrorized as entertainment, especially as I see real terror ahead in the form of existential threats if we cross those planetary boundaries, or accidentally start a nuclear war.

The role of the Talebearer in our Global Collaboratory is to support the emotional and psychological journey to sustainability we need to make. The Talebearers would partner with each of the SDGs' themes being explored to support the creation of transmedia storytelling that could reach beyond the confines of the participating countries and groups to the general populace. For example, we could have a film about a health care collective which despite the many challenges succeeds in defeating the dragons of the moment to put in place a health care system that values people over profits. For years, we have perpetuated the myth of a single superhero coming to save us, but thankfully, the Avengers superheroes, has begun to break that myth. Each of the Avengers has different gifts and talents and they all need to work together to save the world. We need to promote more of this collectivist cosmology so that we can create the subconscious field of thought that will support the evolutionary shift to a sustainability paradigm.

We belong to the Earth. The Earth does not belong to us. This is an evolutionary shift. It happens inside the mind with or without the change of the rules and regulations which define our lifestyles.

The COVIDemic provides an opening. The global economic and financial community is actively looking for new ideas that might accelerate economic and social recovery. Beyond this, many private companies are trying to pivot to a new value system. What if the SMART Futures Global Collaboratory was funded by 30 billionaires who would step forward to put forward $1 billion each to fund the Global Collaboratory, a total of $30 billion, over the next ten years. What if UNESCO and UNDP who are already committed to promoting futures literacy and strategic foresight were to support the training of 30,000 SDG multipliers who would be trained to convene design labs with each of the countries involved in the labs. It is in our reach to imagine training the 5 million connectors who can help us arrive at the 500 million that can help us arrive at a tipping point. There are several professional certification organizations that could also help to imprint a SMART Futures framework into their executive training programming. For example, Lean Six Sigma Certification could be transformed to Sustainable Lean Six Sigma Training. Another example is the Project Management Professional (PMP), which is a highly desirable and recognized certificate globally. There are 932,000 project management certified professionals and 300 chartered chapters in countries and territories worldwide. What if these experts could be provided with exposure to the SMART Futures framework in Project Management? There is no need to create a professional certification for a SMART Futures paradigm. In fact, placing the SMART Futures framework in that model would slow down the adoption of the process. Rather the goal is to reach out to all professional, technical and management organizations to share the vision of the SMART Futures framework as a means to short circuit "silo-ization" and create systems thinkers and problem-solvers.

This approach to establishing the Global Collaboratory could be identified with SDG 17 which is about partnership global consciousness, the capacity and disposition to understand and act upon issues of global significance is at a high state of resonance. SDG 17 states that partnerships are to strengthen the means of implementation and revitalize the Global Partnership for development.

The Global Collaboratory design is based on the philosophy of SDG 17. For us to move to a SMART Futures paradigm, the idea of smart (which means being connected and intelligent) has to be applied to how we think, not just to things like our phones and houses and banks and cars. We have to see ourselves as SMART communities and SMART governments intent on shaping and sharing SMART Futures.

It is beneficial that right now we are in an inflection point in the noosphere. Gen Z is very aware of this hive mind in large part because they are truly digital natives. They are used to being connected and sharing their personal lives online in ways that Boomers don't, from Facebook to Instagram to TikTok, their friends are people they may never meet in the real world. Thus, if the Talebearers take hold of the #SMARTFutures meme and are able to go viral in the "twitterverse," we stand a chance.

Let me clarify that the SMART Futures framework will not result in a uniform world. And a uniform world is not what we desire. For example, if working with Aborigines, consider metrics for economic flourishing, rather than economic development, because development means Western standards which they do not want. In this case, they want to flourish in the construct of what they believe to be fair for all humanity. The quicker we learn that the better it is for us, and the more likely we are to survive. We passed Earth Overshoot Day on Day 234 of the year 2020. We are now living on borrowed time. It is a very important thing that we all have to know about.

Day Seven
The Year 2030
Anansi Checks Out International Human Solidarity Day

December 20, 2030
Voice Journal, Co-Chairs of the Governing Council, Global
Convention of the Ubuntu Alliance

*Today, for the third time, we will file our lawsuit to save the Caribbean
Sea. We are feeling more than optimistic, for win or lose, going forward,
we know we have already won in the court of public opinion. After the
court threw out our suit in 2027, for the second time – we first filed
in 2022 – we have worked tirelessly to secure new followers and to
build our movement. Finding Caribbean Leaders ready to go toe to toe
with the status quo was not an easy road. Were it not for the strong
connections we have made with indigenous peoples around the world
including in the United States and Canada, and the Earth Guardians,
an offshoot of the Children's Climate Movement, that came into being
in 2021 in the wake of the COVID-19 Pandemic, we would not be
here. Although, truth be told, our Ocean Justice League Game should
be given their due. What started out as one man's vision to protect the
Caribbean Sea has yielded a much larger catch than he anticipated.
The Ocean Justice League Game is just one of a suite of games that has
made the Ubuntu Alliance one of the most influential NGOs on the
planet. The games themselves are the lynchpin of a group of companies
in the information, communication and technology space which is our
playing ground or battlefield – depending on your point of view.*

*Crowding round the console at Ubuntu Decision Theater Central
at midnight last night, it was pandemonium when our megahit virtual
reality game hit 100 million unique players around the world. On
this International Human Solidarity Day, we are gathering to lay
the groundwork for what we must do in the coming ten to twenty
years. The success of our gaming platform has enabled us to create
waves of empowered global citizens who have allowed us to harness*

people power and direct it to changemaking. With our community of 100 million people, we are placed among the top five online gaming companies and demonstrated our capability to wield influence among a highly sophisticated user group. As a result, we have demonstrated to both the UN Security Council and the International Aerospace Industry Alliance, which is made up of the top 1000 companies operating across all sectors of the Space industry, that there are masses of people across the world committed to ensuring human rights to access Space. We have gained agreement about issues of Space debris and Space sustainability. As partners of the United Planetary Society to Assure the Rights to Space (UPSTARTS) we were among one of the first 150 NGOs who had signed the petition to ensure Space was treated as a Zone of Peace for all humanity and pushed our member representatives from NGOs from each UN member country to set up local councils at home.

When we launched our gaming initiative back in 2021, we knew that in order for us to survive as an NGO, we had to have an enterprise model. We decided to use games to harness the power of transmedia storytelling – from games to books, comics, music and films. We have succeeded, far surpassing our wildest imaginings of 2021 – developing projects to address issues ranging from the oceans to Space to geo-engineering constructs like "geo-engineered forests" to support carbon capture across Asia. Today, we have amassed a network of over 27,000 scientists, and a consortium of 150 universities of which 130 were from the developing countries in Africa, Asia, the Caribbean, Latin America and the Pacific, and twenty partners handpicked from Australia, China, Europe, Japan, Korea, New Zealand and the United States of America.

In addition to our success with gaming and entertainment division, we have our search engine that is used by over one billion people and ranked in the top ten in the world. Ubuntu Communications is the largest cooperatively owned internet company, and our Cybersecurity Collective has over 10,000 ethical hackers and cyber-guardians. Without them we would not have been able to amass the cyber-power we have today. Between organized criminal forces and repressive state governments, we have had many attempts to disrupt our processes. The control of cyberspace is vital for our bargaining power with state governments and the private sector agents who want to maintain twentieth-century hegemony over the twenty-first-century global economy. Ubuntu Communications' success with internet telecommunications, has led to our taking a stake in energy services and several community owned infrastructure companies for water and waste management in Africa, the Caribbean and the Pacific. Today, our movement has created community-based clones that have contributed to a 50% reduction of poverty around the world.

I am the first to admit that were it not for the 2020 COVID-19 pandemic which provided the opportunity for the reset of processes and policies, we would not have had the freedom to innovate. Many of us in various movements used the chaos of the moment to come together across borders and boundaries to challenge the system in new ways. It was a time of turn around and turning out, a time of inside out and upside down. It was the perfect setting for the birth of the Ubuntu Alliance – our global movement for just futures. Using the SMART Futures paradigm, the founders of our movement used media and entertainment as an entry point to the task of decolonizing the future.

It became clear after COVID-19 that the American Dream could not be the global vision, and the race for the SDGs was retooled and modified to ensure that we lived within the nine scientific planetary boundaries. The Ubuntu SMART Futures Game built on the basis and values of the SMART Futures paradigm, has made the concept of wellbeing and the circular economy common among today's college students. This is driving change in industries across the world. Some have already retrofitted their financial and fiduciary operations to ensure that lifecycle properly accounts for waste and that symbiotic engineering design is followed to promote reduction of waste. Future Generations Wellbeing Acts has been passed into law in over twenty countries in Africa and over thirty members of the 55-member Alliance of Small Island States. Several US States have also adopted wellbeing laws and standards and are creating social services corps that allow for over millions of students to attend college for no interest loans or free while "working" to supplement labor shortages in social and environmental care fields. This includes work as substitute teachers, Mentors, elder care and environmental wardens.

"UBUNTU City of the Future" game launched in 2023 enabled us to test our concepts for inner city America with SMART Futures design labs, and in two years we had over 30 communities and cities in various states of trial. Our climate change critics claimed that we were not doing enough to address the root cause, but by 2028, cities in Colorado, Ohio, Michigan and Pennsylvania who were receiving the influx of climate refugees from New York City; Miami, Florida; and New Orleans, Louisiana, were praising the game as a resource for participatory social design. At the same time, our engineered solutions helped us begin the upgrading of three of Africa's major slums in Nairobi, Johannesburg, and Lagos.

SMART cities are focused on capturing more value from existing infrastructure and "designing out" the impacts of pollution, climate change, toxins and congestion. SMART Cities are focused on defining and securing citizen wellbeing that is assessing social coherence, environmental health and human security alongside the UN Sustainable Development Goals. All in all, the SMART Futures paradigm that has guided our design and development processes in our games and gaming platforms has proven to be able to advance our values of good-faith cooperation, freedom of inquiry, openness and transparency, rigor and integrity, inclusion and reciprocity.

Thinking about the lawsuit ahead, it is our hope that our Ocean Guardians Film, launching on the next June 8, World Ocean Day, along with the games and books will create the conditions for a win. For right now, we are thrilled that a swarm of reporters has camped out outside the courthouse and in less than twelve hours the carnival masquerade band we have commissioned will host a flash party to the hit single from the Games EP collection attracting media attention upwards of four million people. If it takes fun and games to win this war, so be it. Humanity must come to recognize our collective responsibility to protect the Earth, the climate, the cosmos. What's next? The work has only just begun. Today, International Human Solidarity Day is a day to celebrate our unity in diversity; to remind governments to respect their commitments to international agreements; to promote the utilization of cooperative approaches to meeting the challenges of growing inequality; to raise public awareness of the importance of the achievement of the Sustainable Development Goals for our thrival; to advance human rights, social and economic justice and above all collective peace and security in our shared futures. A Luta Continua.

Chapter 7

What Can You Do to Be Partner or Midwife to the New Future?

If you are reading this book, you, like me, have most likely chosen to see the opportunity of the Great Pause created by the pandemic as a period of gestation as opposed to a period of stagnation. We know we can't go back to what was. We can't build back better. We can only go forward to something different, the future we want... a future of flourishing. Eudaimonia not utopia. Eudaimonia is not a state of happiness in the mind for the individual, but instead an objective standard of what it means to flourish as humans because we hold as a virtue the capacity to reason well. So "How can we midwife this eudaimonia? How can we be the change that we want to see?" We all belong to some clan or tribe: our academic community, our high school community, the professional communities such as engineering, social work, medical, health care, manufacturing. What WE as a community might want looks very different for each of us. We find that sometimes the communities that we belong to are in conflict, as WE the people (in the marine parks community) have a different vision of the future of the sea from WE the people (in the oil and gas industry). Yet, WE each and every one of the us in these communities all fundamentally want the same thing: a thriving life for ourselves and our communities of interest. We want clean water, energy, proper sanitation, decent housing, nutritious food, affordable healthcare, good jobs. Whether we are in highly underdeveloped, moderately burdened, or least entangled (HUMBLE) nations ranging from Argentina to Laos, Mozambique, Singapore or Zambia; or in the Western, educated, industrialized, rich, developed (WEIRD) countries like Australia, Canada, or Germany, we want the same thing: thriving futures. We all want for our children and grandchildren to live a life equal to or better than the life that we have lived. We want to flourish.

It is challenging to think about 2050 when we don't even know what the next month and next year will be like. We recognize that most of us live better today, with longer life expectancy and better teeth than we did some 100 years ago. If we were able to travel to the year 3000, like Anansi, given we can look back on the year 1000, what is it we would wish the history books to say of life then? Will we be considered good ancestors? Would they say that back in 2030 the people were wise enough to find a way or make a way to turn our destiny as humanity in the direction of "thrival"? Is there a moral law that says we should care?

I like to believe that if we can send a probe to the sun, then we certainly ought to able to ensure nobody goes hungry. I like to believe that if you are reading this book then you care about our human condition and you believe in our capacity for change and that you are looking for your guidance possibility system to direct your path. You understand yourself as an interdependent being in this mesh of life and that the hornets' nest of challenges belongs to all of us, and demands that we, all of us, cross the borders and boundaries we have placed on ourselves and each other so that we can cultivate change.

Let's do a thought experiment. If I were to say to you, "What is the change you would like to see in the year 2030?" Is it equal opportunity to good education for all children in inner city America, or sanitation for people in rural Asia, or health care for people in rural Africa or Appalachia? What is it that you would like to see? Where do you see yourself in this story? Ask yourself, what is the gap between your life story and the story of the future that you want to see? If you have been able to identify a future that you want clearly, then can you identify the gap between your life story and that future story? Can you see yourself in that future story? If not, what experience is keeping you from playing a role in the future story? Is it that you think you are too small, you don't have any power, or is it that you are thinking, I have no time for that now, or that is not my responsibility, or I wouldn't know where to start, or I have no expertise in this area? What is the belief that you hold that keeps you from being the change you want to see? What advice you would give to your newborn niece, godchild, grandchild, son, daughter born in this decade? For whatever advice you give that child would be relevant to the story you want to create to ensure human thriving at the end of the twenty-first century.

And given your sphere of influence, how can you get more people to see themselves in our global story and recognize that we all are co-creating a shared future? For example, the average American seems unaware of the SDGs. Considering the level of inequality in America, this is a conundrum that demands care and repair: "What if more Americans would see the SDGs as a rallying point and take on SDG 4 to push for affordable health care for all; or SDG 3 Education or SDG 10 for Inequality or SDG 13 Climate Action in the local communities and cities? What if the different movements: climate, environmental justice, health care, living wage, labor, children's right, corporate rights movement were to join hands around the SDGs and co-create a shared narrative for an American wellbeing movement that drives us forward together, a SMART America movement?

It is clearly a failure in imagining our futures that has led to our seeming inability to design solutions to address these challenges already. We look at SDG 10 which addresses inequality and the links to racial and ethnic discrimination and wonder how we might end mass incarceration and disrupt the public-school-to-prison pipeline for black people, Native Americans, Hispanics. If we were able to put a man on the moon with black women serving as human calculators when they were still not accepted in certain schools or cafeterias, there is absolutely no reason to believe that a goal of 100% completion of quality grade-12 education by the year 2030 is too much to ask. Can we have early childhood daycare that has education and support services for a full 100% of children? Are these goals too much to hope for?

You don't need to be "THE" Leader of the movement. It is enough to be "A" follower in the movement. According to my homespun theory of movements, aka "movementology," for a transformational change to take hold, the followers (not just the Leaders) must see themselves as change-makers. Somewhere out there is a movement that needs you to help take it forward. How do you start? By recognizing that the power to change the world resides in each and every one of us. The power is in our hands, as we are all connected to the world through the power of the SMART phones, we carry with us. This is the currency of distributed power. Power that is held by the many as opposed to the few. While the old power movements were command and control from the top of the pyramid, new power is about sharing the passion and vision and recognizing that we are co-creating our futures. In the old days, only a few were chosen and invited to the table. Today we can create new tables, draw new circles, build new apps. We are moving from the adage "the revolution will be televised" to "the evolution will be telecommunicated." And the evolution will lead to the various transformational changes needed to take us to SMART Futures.

Within every heart there is wisdom waiting to be awakened through our personal evolution. How do we undertake this awakening? How do we access right thinking, right feelings, right words, right action, right reactions – five principles?

Right-thinking, unlocked by your spiritual intelligence will allow you to see that we are each a living ecosystem embedded in a complex of living and man-made ecosystems.

Right feelings, our second principle, is the moral intelligence that allows us to recognize we must have Meaningful Metrics based on the moral law that recognizes that we are interdependent beings, and altruism is a principle and a practice that ensures the happiness of other human beings as well as the animal kingdom. That in which we live, results in a better quality of life for all of us.

Right words, the third principle requires us to apply our analytical and aspirational intelligence. In order to design for a thriving future, we must recognize our agency and use our analytical and aspirational intelligence to assure both adaptive and Anticipatory Agency. Without aspiration our analysis might suffer from a failure of imagination. Without analytical intelligence we might find ourselves failing in ability to adapt.

Right action, the fourth principle is unlocked by our relational intelligence, both inter and intra-personal. Intra-personal intelligence is that capacity to explore our own inner world and feel it. While inter-personal intelligence is about the capacity to understand others, to work with others, to have empathy for others, to have social intelligence. We need these in order to behave in ways that allow us to be with others in such a way that we can really have personal resilience and social resilience. Things will go wrong. We must have emotional resonance and relational intelligence that drive us to right actions.

Right reactions, the fifth principle, are unlocked by our temporal intelligence. How we understand time is based on our culture. We recognize that this requires us to understand that the future is not yet written; it requires us to understand and have temporal intelligence; it requires us to be able to understand the past to learn from the past and bring it in to the present. Temporal intelligence allows us to understand first, second and third order consequences of our actions. To see the ripples in the pond that we cause far out into the lake. It's about having the right reaction to things that are emerging. To be aware that past, present and future exist in some way in the same moment. Temporal intelligence allows us to harness the power of our vision, our dreams, our images of the future and respond appropriately.

We have to begin to transform ourselves from the rabidly individualistic culture where people are considered to be good if they're strong, self-reliant, assertive, and independent, to people who seek the balance needed in recognizing our interdependence. To understand that being self-sacrificing, dependable, generous, and helpful to others are of equal if not greater importance than our old myths of individualism, especially now. Collectivist cultures are more common in Africa and Asia where families and communities have a central role, and the social norms focus on promoting selflessness. But we in the WEIRD, Western, educated, individualistic, rich, developed countries can change and become more collectivistic in our ways of being. We saw that the crisis of the COVIDemic revealed all sides of the coin. For some, it brought out the better angels of our nature. While for others, it brought forth anger and fear. Many wanted to "Live free or die!" While others simply remain in observation mode. Immobilized by worry, anxiety, and lack of direction.

Your choice is to listen to the still, small voice and start from where you are. Take the first step, where you work, where you volunteer, where you play, where you worship.

Finally, the principle of Sankofa, which says "it is not wrong for us to go back and fetch that which you might have forgotten" should be noted. There is much need for intergenerational dialogue. Much could be gained by bringing in the wisdom of the past with the wisdom of the future – those Leaders who have gone before and the children emerging to lead us now. The Hebrew phrase (from the Jewish tradition) of Tikkun Olam can be translated to "repair of the world." We are being called on to repair the world now so that we can thrive. The transformation of our way of being in the world is our sacred duty to ourselves, generations to come, our Earth Mother and Father Time.

Ask yourself, "What is sacred to me?" What would you

change in your life if they told you that you were going to die in the next 20 years? If you knew, in fact, that you would be dead in the next 10 years, what would you do? What is the legacy that you want to leave? This question can help you identify what is really sacred to you. Perhaps answering that question will make us identify what truly matters and help us clarify the story about the future we want and our place in it.

In sharing my vision of a world empowered by a SMART Futures mindset, it is my hope that the process outlined in the five questions becomes the seeds of a new meme and the gospel of a new global movement for thrival. If it takes ten percent of the world population to make a new way of being stick, then the SMART Futures mindset and tools will need to become as commonplace as Google or Microsoft or smartphones. It is hoped that you will become a vector for this paradigm shift through the embrace of the power of spiritual, moral, analytical-aspirational, relational and temporal intelligence in you, to make the change you want to see, and to be the changemaker you must be.

We belong to this Earth and the Cosmos. It is ours to share, to steward, to explore for generations to come, until time winds down. The stories we tell about our future now will be the foundation stones for what we build. It will take a renewal of mind to bring forth the right thinking, right feelings, right words, right action and right reaction needed to meet the challenges of the sustainable development goals and beyond. We have one choice and that is to move forward toward the hope we most deeply desire.

On this spaceship Earth, there are no passengers. We are all crew. Your choice to evolve will demand more of you, perhaps more than anything you have done before. You will have to travel in uncharted waters that will not always be smooth sailing. The purpose of the SMART Futures paradigm enshrined in these five questions is to help us make transformational shifts necessary. Can five questions really make a difference? Just think how many marvels and mysteries have been unraveled or discovered because someone asked the right question. It is my belief that the SMART Futures Paradigm is the key to open the door to the futures we want, by helping us to co-create the changes we wish to see. Are you ready to engender a flourishing world for all? May it be so.

How Humans Were Saved from Extinction: Is Anansi Mek It

"KRIK!" (And you say "KRAK!")

And it came to pass that as the days sped by... Anansi soon realized that there is no way he was going to be able to collect enough stories all by himself in order to show Chaos and his posse that humans were worthy of saving, because there were just too many places and times when humans envisioned thrival and not survival. He decided to get help from his cousins – Grandmother Spider and her sisters all across the Earth from time past to time present and yet to come, who were also well known for their skills in weaving: The Great Norns – Urðr, Verðandi and Skuld; The Moraie; and the Nesoi – who looked after the affairs of islands. He tasked his Spider Woman Posse to collect stories of the good and plenty that demonstrated humans' use of knowledge and common sense to aid him in showing the Gods that seeds of hope for futures of flourishing were all around.

So, they collected stories from everywhere and everywhen, from all corners of the Earth and the Galaxy, and all across the aeons of time, and heaped them up to be presented to the conclave of the Gods. By the by, the clock was ticking, and Anansi decided it best to collect the stories, the seeds of hope for human futures into his calabash. But, as it turned out, one calabash was not enough. So, he needed to find another and another and another and another... and though his time was running out, still the stories kept coming, and piling up. What was Anansi to do? How to carry all these seeds of hope? How to best present the best of the best? Where was he to store them? As he pondered his quandary, he heard the voice of Chaos bellowing, "Time's Up!" And then the chorus began "Time's Up. Time's Up. Time's up." Anansi stood stock still. Every part of his body was quivering and itching as he thought and scratched furiously. Grandmother Spider noticing his freeze and seeing the pile of calabashes, understood their dilemma.

"KRIK!" (And You say "KRAK!")

In an instant, inspiration struck. She said, "Why not hang the calabash from the limbs of the Yggdrasil tree? And so stealthily, Anansi and the Spider Woman posse began to weave strings to connect the calabash to the Yggdrasil tree, working as quickly as they could. The chorus grew louder. "Time's Up!" Time's up!" "Time's up!" Anansi replied, "Ah Soon Come." Time's Up! Time's Up!" The increasingly insistent sound of the Gods chanting was now creating a windstorm. "Ah coming just now," Anansi screeched frantically. "ANANSI!" The voice of Chaos thundered in his ear. Lightning flashed as Chaos, angry at being ignored, hurled a bolt at Anansi's feet. In his shock, Anansi dropped the calabash he was about to hang, and stories of hope came tumbling out in a kaleidoscope of color. And where the lighting struck the earth, a spring of water bubbled forth. That is why tongue has it to say, "Hope springs eternal." And as for the Reasoning of the Conclave? Well, my friends, the rest of this story is for another day. For, the world is a story without a beginning we tell to each other, from the day that we're born to the day that we die. And now the story is yours.

"KRIK!" (And you say "KRAK!")

TO BE CONTINUED...

References

Chapter One

"Africa: Amnesty Report on Human Rights - Africa 2016/2017 - AllAfrica.Com." Accessed July 5, 2021. https://allafrica.com/stories/201702220437.html.

"Anthropocene | National Geographic Society." Accessed July 5, 2021. https://www.nationalgeographic.org/encyclopedia/anthropocene/.

Butler, Octavia. *Parable of the Talents.* New York, NY: Grand Central Publishing, 2019. https://www.scribd.com/book/171096156/Parable-of-the-Talents.

"COVID-19 Is Increasing Multiple Kinds of Inequality | World Economic Forum." Accessed July 5, 2021. https://www.weforum.org/agenda/2020/10/covid-19-is-increasing-multiple-kinds-of-inequality-here-s-what-we-can-do-about-it/.

"Earth's $40-Billion Weather Disasters of 2019: 4th Most Billion-Dollar Events on Record - Scientific American Blog Network." Accessed July 5, 2021. https://blogs.scientificamerican.com/eye-of-the-storm/earths-40-billion-dollar-weather-disasters-of-2019-4th-most-billion-dollar-events-on-record/.

"Existential Risk - Future of Life Institute." Accessed July 5, 2021. https://futureoflife.org/background/existential-risk/.

"Fact of the Month - Word of the Week | Knowledge Hub." Accessed July 5, 2021. https://knowledge.unccd.int/knowledge-products-and-pillars/unccd-e-library/fact-month-word-week.

"FAO - News Article: Declining Bee Populations Pose Threat to Global Food Security and Nutrition." Accessed July 5, 2021. http://www.fao.org/news/story/en/item/1194910/icode/.

"Fourth Industrial Revolution - Wikipedia." Accessed July 5, 2021. https://en.wikipedia.org/wiki/Fourth_Industrial_Revolution.

Frost and Sullivan. "EXPERIENCING CITY LIFE IN 2030: TRENDS & PERSPECTIVES." *Dassamunt Systemes*, n.d., 38.

"Have We Crossed the 9 Planetary Boundaries?" Accessed July 5, 2021. https://news.climate.columbia.edu/2011/08/05/have-we-crossed-the-9-planetary-boundaries/.

"Home | Fight Inequality." Accessed July 5, 2021. https://www.fightinequality.org/.

"How Many People Have Smartphones? [Jul 2021 Update] | Oberlo." Accessed July 5, 2021. https://www.oberlo.com/statistics/how-many-people-have-smartphones.

"If Solar Panels Are So Clean, Why Do They Produce So Much Toxic Waste?" Accessed July 5, 2021. https://www.forbes.com/sites/michaelshellenberger/2018/05/23/if-solar-panels-are-so-clean-why-do-they-produce-so-much-toxic-waste/?sh=208a5db0121c.

"Key Drivers and Research Challenges for 6G Ubiquitous Wireless Intelligence (White Paper)." Accessed July 5, 2021. https://www.researchgate.net/publication/336000008_Key_drivers_and_research_challenges_for_6G_ubiquitous_wireless_intelligence_white_paper.

"Natural Resources: Are We Blessed with a Curse or Cursed with a Blessing? | News24." Accessed July 5, 2021. https://www.news24.com/news24/MyNews24/natural-resources-are-we-blessed-with-a-curse-or-are-we-cursed-with-a-blessing-20170508.

"Op-Ed Archives - Page 24 of 1775 - Daily Times." Accessed July 5, 2021. https://dailytimes.com.pk/opeds/page/24/.

"Permafrost Melt Is Now Contributing to Climate Change Emissions - Vox." Accessed July 5, 2021. https://www.vox.com/energy-and-environment/2019/12/12/21011445/permafrost-melting-arctic-report-card-noaa.

"RayGator's Swamp Gas | Swamp Gas Forums." Accessed July 5, 2021. https://www.gatorcountry.com/swampgas/forums/raygators-swamp-gas.5/.

"Refugee Statistics | USA for UNHCR." Accessed July 5, 2021. https://www.unrefugees.org/refugee-facts/statistics/.

"Samuel Huntington's 'Bloody Borders' Revisited | Andrew Holt, Ph.D." Accessed July 5, 2021. https://apholt.com/2016/05/28/ samuel-huntingtons-bloody-borders-revisited/.

" Solar Panels Tires | Simplifying Energy." Accessed July 5, 2021. http://simplifyingenergy.com/?s=solar+panels+tires.

"Sunhak Peace Prize." Accessed July 5, 2021. http:// sunhakpeaceprize.org/en/index.php.

"The 2030 Agenda for Sustainable Development: Transforming Education." Accessed July 5, 2021. https://blog.storymirror. com/read/byn9node/transforming-education.

"The Dark Side of Natural Resources." Accessed July 5, 2021. https://archive.globalpolicy.org/dark-side-of-natural-resources.html.

"The Mining of Coltan: Chances Are Your Smartphone Was Manufactured With African Blood." Accessed July 5, 2021. https://atlantablackstar.com/2017/09/25/mining-coltan-chances-smartphone-manufactured-african-blood/.

"The Moon, Mars and Beyond… the Space Race in 2020 | Space | The Guardian." Accessed July 5, 2021. https://www. theguardian.com/science/2020/jan/05/space-race-moon-mars-asteroids-commercial-launches.

"The World's Living Creatures Are Disappearing at Unprecedented Rates - Here's What We Stand to Lose, According to a Landmark UN Report | BusinessInsider India." Accessed July 5, 2021. https://www.businessinsider. in/miscellaneous/the-worlds-living-creatures-are-disappearing-at-unprecedented-rates-heres-what-we-stand-to-lose-according-to-a-landmark-un-report/ slidelist/69224751.cms.

"University of Essex - Guest Blog: Tell Us Your Views on Our Draft Digital, Creative and Cultural Sub-Strategy « Vice-Chancellor." Accessed July 5, 2021. http://blogs.essex.ac.uk/

vc/2017/03/23/digitalcreative/.

Weltwirtschaftsforum and Zurich Insurance Group. *Global Risks 2019: Insight Report*, 2019. http://www3.weforum.org/docs/WEF_Global_Risks_Report_2019.pdf.

"What Is the Ecological Footprint? - Earth Overshoot Day." Accessed July 5, 2021. https://www.overshootday.org/kids-and-teachers-corner/what-is-an-ecological-footprint/.

"World Defence Spending Continues Upward–But COVID-19 | Mark Collins 3Ds Blog." Accessed July 5, 2021. https://mark3ds.wordpress.com/2020/04/27/world-defence-spending-continues-upward-but-covid-19/.

"World Urbanization Prospects | Blog | Eunetwork.Lv." Accessed July 5, 2021. https://eunetwork.lv/blog/2018/06/world-urbanization-prospects.

"World's Billionaires Have More Wealth than 4.6 Billion People | Oxfam International." Accessed July 5, 2021. https://www.oxfam.org/en/press-releases/worlds-billionaires-have-more-wealth-46-billion-people.

"World's Billionaires Have More Wealth than 4.6 Billion People | Oxfam Philippines." Accessed July 5, 2021. https://philippines.oxfam.org/latest/press-release/world%E2%80%99s-billionaires-have-more-wealth-46-billion-people.

Chapter Two

"Achieving SDGs in Zambia – Zambia Daily Mail." Accessed July 5, 2021. http://www.daily-mail.co.zm/achieving-sdgs-in-zambia/.

"Background on Energy & Oil." Accessed July 5, 2021. https://ontheissues.org/Background_Energy_+_Oil.htm.

"GROWING SUSTAINABILITY - PDF Free Download." Accessed July 5, 2021. http://docplayer.net/44468192-Growing-sustainability.html.

"How the COVID-19 Pandemic Has Changed Americans'

Personal Lives | Pew Research Center." Accessed July 5, 2021. https://www.pewresearch.org/2021/03/05/in-their-own-words-americans-describe-the-struggles-and-silver-linings-of-the-covid-19-pandemic/.

"ICSB Staff | ICSB | International Council for Small Business." Accessed July 5, 2021. https://icsb.org/author/icsbioadmin/page/41/.

Kendi, Ibram X. *How to Be an Antiracist*. First Edition. New York: One World, 2019.

"Nation-States and Sovereignty | Boundless World History." Accessed July 5, 2021. https://courses.lumenlearning.com/boundless-worldhistory/chapter/nation-states-and-sovereignty/.

"Paris Climate Agreement to Enter into Force on 4 November – United Nations Sustainable Development." Accessed July 5, 2021. https://www.un.org/sustainabledevelopment/blog/2016/10/paris-climate-agreement-to-enter-into-force-on-4-november/.

"Powering Ahead." Accessed July 5, 2021. https://mbrf.ae/en/read/city-of-the-future/9.

"Richest Nations Agree to End Support for Coal Production Overseas | Coal | The Guardian." Accessed July 5, 2021. https://www.theguardian.com/environment/2021/may/21/richest-nations-agree-to-end-support-for-coal-production-overseas.

"The Paris Agreement - Library Records - OD Mekong Datahub." Accessed July 5, 2021. https://data.opendevelopmentmekong.net/dataset/the-paris-agreement.

"The Peace of Westphalia and Sovereignty | Western Civilization." Accessed July 5, 2021. https://courses.lumenlearning.com/suny-hccc-worldhistory/chapter/the-peace-of-westphalia-and-sovereignty/.

"The Rise And Fall Of Japan Over The Deadly Mauritius Oil Spill." Accessed July 5, 2021. https://www.forbes.com/sites/

nishandegnarain/2020/12/11/the-rise-and-fall-of-japan-over-the-deadly-mauritius-oil-spill/?sh=310fa70e1e87.

"Tradehero.Mobi." Accessed July 5, 2021. http://ww7.tradehero.mobi/.

"Vail Law: Origins of Our Religious Freedoms | VailDaily.Com." Accessed July 5, 2021. https://www.vaildaily.com/news/vail-law-origins-of-our-religious-freedoms/.

"What's New @ SWC Library?: 2016." Accessed July 5, 2021. http://swcwhatsnew.blogspot.com/2016/.

"World Population Projections - Worldometer." Accessed July 5, 2021. https://www.worldometers.info/world-population/world-population-projections/.

Chapter Three

"Judeo-Christian Religion's Impact on Humans' Attitudes Towards Their Environment." Accessed July 5, 2021. http://fubini.swarthmore.edu/~ENVS2/sierra/Essay2.html.

"Maximizing Uptime in Mission- Critical Facilities - PDF Free Download." Accessed July 5, 2021. http://docplayer.net/18706931-Maximizing-uptime-in-mission-critical-facilities.html.

"Minority Rules: Scientists Discover Tipping Point for the Spread of Ideas | News & Events." Accessed July 5, 2021. https://news.rpi.edu/luwakkey/2902.

Chapter Four

Allen, James. *As a Man Thinketh*. Accessed July 5, 2021. https://moam.info/as-a-man-sic-thinketh-irish-secure_5a22f4eb1723ddcb6f51c013.html.

"Association Insights Archives - Page 2 of 12 - Velvet Chainsaw." Accessed July 5, 2021. https://velvetchainsaw.com/category/association-insights/page/2/.

"Future Generations: Commissioner for Wales Annual Report 2017-2018," n.d. https://senedd.wales/laid%20documents/

gen-ld11694/gen-ld11694-e.pdf.

"Juliana v. United States - Wikipedia." Accessed July 5, 2021. https://en.wikipedia.org/wiki?curid=56263501.

"Learning and Development Are Interdependent, But They're Not the Same Thing | 5D Development." Accessed July 5, 2021. https://5ddevelopment.com/2017/09/24/learning-and-development-are-interdependent-but-theyre-not-the-same-thing/.

"Mental Rehearsal Prepares Our Brains For Real World Actions - Neuroscience News." Accessed July 5, 2021. https://neurosciencenews.com/mental-rehearsal-action-8505/.

"Perspective: Sharing Authors' Quotes on Enrichment and Growth." Accessed July 5, 2021. https://www.newstribune.com/news/news/story/2014/dec/14/perspective-sharing-authors-quotes-enrichment-and-/457715/.

"Play for Wales (Autumn 2016 Issue 47) by Play Wales - Issuu." Accessed July 5, 2021. https://issuu.com/playwales/docs/play_for_wales_autumn_2016_issue_47?e=53.

"Teleological Design – Definition and Weaknesses – The Weblog of (a) David Jones." Accessed July 5, 2021. https://davidtjones.wordpress.com/2009/06/05/teleological-design-definition-and-weaknesses/.

Universal Foundation for Better Living, Inc. "OUR BELIEFS – The Nature of God." Accessed July 5, 2021. https://ufbl.org/our-beliefs/.

"Unravelling the DNA of Knowledge." Accessed July 5, 2021. http://www.geocities.ws/paideusis/e1n2al.html.

Chapter Five

"3 Principles for Developing Metrics | Thinking Strategically: The Appropriate Use of Metrics for the Climate Change Science Program | The National Academies Press." Accessed July 5, 2021. https://www.nap.edu/read/11292/chapter/5.

"Guide to the Systems Engineering Body of Knowledge."

Accessed July 5, 2021. https://www.sebokwiki.org/wiki/ SEBoK_Table_of_Contents.

McKinsey & Company. "Six Problem Solving Mindsets for Very Uncertain Times." Accessed July 5, 2021. https://www. mckinsey.com/business-functions/strategy-and-corporate-finance/our-insights/six-problem-solving-mindsets-for-very-uncertain-times#.

"Resilience for Life | Actualise Daily." Accessed July 5, 2021. https://actualisedaily.com/life/resilience-life/.

"Rights of Nature | CELDF | Championing Nature & Communities." Accessed July 5, 2021. https://celdf.org/ rights-of-nature/.

Chapter Six

Khan, Farid. "Rehabilitation for the Realisation of Human Rights and Inclusive Development," n.d., 44.

"Navigating the SDGs: A Business Guide to Engaging with the UN Global Goals," n.d., 96.

"Nurturing Global Consciousness - Extended Essay - LibGuides at United World College Changshu." Accessed July 5, 2021. https://uwcchina.libguides.com/c. php?g=896491&p=6553802.

"Summit Charts New Era of Sustainable Development – United Nations Sustainable Development." Accessed July 5, 2021. https://www.un.org/sustainabledevelopment/blog/2015/09/ summit-charts-new-era-of-sustainable-development-world-leaders-to-gavel-universal-agenda-to-transform-our-world-for-people-and-planet/.

Chapter Seven

"Individualistic Cultures and Behavior." Accessed July 5, 2021. https://www.verywellmind.com/what-are-individualistic-cultures-2795273.

SOUNDTRACK PLAYLIST

Steel Pulse (A Who Responsible)

Jimmy Cliff (Save Our Planet Earth)

Steelpulse (Islands Unite)

Jimmy Cliff (You Can Get It)

Steel Pulse (Wild Goose Chase)

Bob Marley (Exodus)

Bob Marley (Revolution)

Damian Marley (Life is a Circle)

Bob Marley (Heathen)

Chronixx (Legend)

Rastaman Vibrations, Bob Marley

Steel Pulse (Chant a Psalm)

Steel Pulse (Don't Be Afraid)

Chronixx (Do It Fe De Love)

Bob Marley (Redemption Song)

Lila Ike (Where I'm Coming From)

Claire Nelson as Sagient Futurist (Green Revolution on Soundcloud)

Claire Nelson as Sagient Futurist (We Are The Crazy Ones on Soundcloud)

Protoje (Truths and Rights)

Bob Marley (Get Up Stand Up)

TRANSFORMATION

The *Resilience* Series

The Resilience Series is a collaborative effort by the authors of Changemakers Books in response to the 2020 coronavirus epidemic. Each concise volume offers expert advice and practical exercises for mastering specific skills and abilities. Our intention is that by strengthening your resilience, you can better survive and even thrive in a time of crisis.
www.resilience-books.com

Adapt and Plan for the New Abnormal – in the COVID-19 Coronavirus Pandemic
Gleb Tsipursky

Aging with Vision, Hope and Courage in a Time of Crisis
John C. Robinson

Connecting with Nature in a Time of Crisis
Melanie Choukas-Bradley

Going Within in a Time of Crisis
P. T. Mistlberger

Grow Stronger in a Time of Crisis
Linda Ferguson

Handling Anxiety in a Time of Crisis
George Hoffman

Navigating Loss in a Time of Crisis
Jules De Vitto

The Life-Saving Skill of Story
Michelle Auerbach

Virtual Teams – Holding the Center When You Can't Meet Face-to-Face
Carlos Valdes-Dapena

Virtually Speaking – Communicating at a Distance
Tim Ward and Teresa Erickson

Current Bestsellers from Changemakers Books

Pro Truth
A Practical Plan for Putting Truth Back into Politics
Gleb Tsipursky and Tim Ward

How can we turn back the tide of post-truth politics, fake news, and misinformation that is damaging our democracy? In the lead up to the 2020 US Presidential Election, Pro Truth provides the answers.

An Antidote to Violence
Evaluating the Evidence
Barry Spivack and Patricia Anne Saunders

It's widely accepted that Transcendental Meditation can create peace for the individual, but can it create peace in society as a whole? And if it can, what could possibly be the mechanism?

Finding Solace at Theodore Roosevelt Island
Melanie Choukas-Bradley

A woman seeks solace on an urban island paradise in Washington D.C. through 2016–17, and the shock of the Trump election.

the bottom
a theopoetic of the streets
Charles Lattimore Howard

An exploration of homelessness fusing theology, jazz-verse and intimate storytelling into a challenging, raw and beautiful tale.

The Soul of Activism
A Spirituality for Social Change
Shmuly Yanklowitz
A unique examination of the power of interfaith spirituality to
fuel the fires of progressive activism.

Future Consciousness
The Path to Purposeful Evolution
Thomas Lombardo
An empowering evolutionary vision of wisdom and the human
mind to guide us in creating a positive future.

Preparing for a World that Doesn't Exist – Yet
Rick Smyre and Neil Richardson
This book is about an emerging Second Enlightenment and the
capacities you will need to achieve success in this new, fast-
evolving world.